By_____

D0403433

LISTENING TO THE BEES

NIGHTWOOD EDITIONS
2018

LISTENING
TO THE
BEES

 MARK L. WINSTON
&
RENÉE SAROJINI SAKLIKAR

1 2 3 4 5 — 22 21 20 19 18

Nightwood Editions
P.O. Box 1779
Gibsons, BC VON 1VO
Canada
www.nightwoodeditions.com

COVER DESIGN & TYPOGRAPHY: Carleton Wilson
COVER & INTERIOR ART: creativemarket.com

Nightwood Editions acknowledges the support of the Canada Council for the Arts, which last year invested $153 million to bring the arts to Canadians throughout the country. We also gratefully acknowledge financial support from the Government of Canada and from the Province of British Columbia through the BC Arts Council and the Book Publishing Tax Credit.

This book has been produced on 100% post-consumer recycled, ancient-forest-free paper, processed chlorine-free and printed with vegetable-based dyes.

Printed and bound in Canada.

LIBRARY AND ARCHIVES CANADA CATALOGUING IN PUBLICATION

Winston, Mark L., author
Listening to the bees / Mark Winston, Renée Saklikar.

Issued in print and electronic formats.
ISBN 978-0-88971-346-8 (hardcover).--ISBN 978-0-88971-131-0 (ebook)

1. Environmentalism. I. Saklikar, Renée Sarojini, 1962-, author II. Title.

GE195.W56 2018 333.72   C2017-905548-8   C2017-905549-6

CONTENTS

Doing science is not such a barrier to feeling or such a dehumanizing influence as is often made out. It does not take the beauty from nature. The only rules of scientific method are honest observations and accurate logic ... No one should feel that honesty and accuracy guided by imagination have any power to take away nature's beauty.

—Robert H. MacArthur, *Geographical Ecology*

l'amor che move il sole e l'altre stelle.

Love that moves—the sun—other stars—

—Dante, *Paradiso*, 33.143–45

PREFACE

I'M SITTING IN MY HOME OFFICE EARLY IN THE MORNING, MY FAVOURITE time for writing. We live in Vancouver's West End, a dense community located at the edge of Stanley Park, with its large expanse of gardens, recreational fields, beaches and urban forest. Our apartment is in a three-storey wood-frame building constructed in 1948, a time when apartment residences were known as much by their names as their addresses. We're "The Belmanor," with fourteen apartments and no elevator.

It's what they call a "character" building, but not at all rundown. Historically, the residents have kept it in impeccable condition. Belmanor's frame was constructed with remarkably thick wooden beams of a girth no longer easy to find, providing an underlying sense of permanence and craftsmanship. Our ancient hot water heating, quirky plumbing system and sixty-amp electrical wiring all date back to the middle of the last century, adding to the building's charm. We've developed good relationships with tradesmen intrigued by working on the historic guts of a building from a bygone era.

We're a cooperative, with a culture of residents each contributing work to maintain our shared space. Belmanor's collective values are particularly visible in the profuse gardens that take up every bit of the small land in front and on the sides of the building, as well as up on the roof. Gardening is very much a communal effort. Lori does the rooftop, Donna and Joan the small side yard, Yolande the showpiece front garden that faces the street, Lorne and Eliot take care of their penthouse garden, and David maintains a few pots in the back alley.

Our gardeners have been conscientious about planting bee-friendly flowers. Blooming in late June as I write today are clover, thyme, oregano, strawberries, tomatoes, rhododendron, cranesbill, oriental poppies, columbine, cornflower, foxglove, hollyhock and lobelia, ensuring that we can enjoy the buzz of pollinating bees. Wild bees abound, including an array of bumblebees and numerous leafcutter, mason, mining and sweat bee species. Honeybees are also abundant, from the many hives managed by beekeepers even in downtown Vancouver. Vancouver neighbourhoods are havens for bees, which benefit from mild winters, a long February-to-October growing season and a ban on most pesticide use. For me it's particularly soothing to live in an apartment and a city surrounded by plants and bees during a time when bees—managed and wild—have been collapsing globally due to human impact on their world.

I find it particularly difficult to see the bees disappearing, as I've spent a forty-year career listening to what the bees can teach us. The ear through which I've listened to bees has been scientific research more than beekeeping, although I've become a pretty fair beekeeper along the way. Research provides a focused methodology with a distinctive rigour through which to learn about bees and their societies, but alone is not sufficient to reveal what the bees can teach us.

Contemporary science tends to the mechanistic and reductionist, focused on the how rather than the why, the parts more than the whole. It wasn't always that way. The word "scientist" didn't even exist until 1834, when English historian and philosopher William Whewell coined the term in a sarcastic article decrying the then-expanding tendency of science to separate from its philosophical origins and be directed more narrowly to functional studies rather than the deeper questions of life.

Natural philosophy preceded science by thousands of years, its practitioners studying nature not only for facts and information but also for the spiritual gleanings and philosophical undertones that address reflective questions about our relationship to the natural and physical spheres, and to each other. The strength of science is in its exacting hypothesis testing and experimentation, which itself is a form of beauty. Its weakness is when it stops there rather than probing further, through the layers of information, into a more profound appreciation of the world around us. Bees provide superb opportunities for that subterranean layer of reflection, because some species have complex societies as social as our own. And all bees have coevolved with plants, expressing the fundamental interdependence of living things.

Today, there is an urgent economic imperative to listen to the bees, since we depend on them for our own survival and prosperity. Without these pollinators, much of our food would not exist, and the habitats we depend on would similarly become wastelands.

Research in my laboratory and with colleagues over the last four decades has addressed a wide array of issues. My earliest work focused on understanding the evolution of social behaviour, the behavioural and ecological reasons for the success of the African "killer" bees in South America, honeybee colony life history and the factors underlying swarming behaviour.

Once I established my own laboratory at Canada's Simon Fraser University in Vancouver, the research shifted to aspects of pheromone communication, honeybee management and ways to enhance crop pollination with both honeybees and wild bees. We eventually added studies of bee diseases and pests as well as factors influencing wild bee diversity and abundance to our research repertoire. These studies were engaging in themselves, but also provided the opportunity to expand the science in the manner of the natural philosophers. I began to ask what else we might learn by listening to the bees, and have been writing and speaking on this subject to public audiences throughout much of my career.

Listening to the Bees is a collaborative exploration by two writers who share a common passion for bees and language. While my interest in bees grew through scientific research, Renée collects poems about bees, intrigued by bees themselves and by the possibilities inherent in the language of science. Renée's preoccupation with bees literally began at birth, when her paternal grandparents conducted the ancient Vedic ritual of anointing her forehead with honey. In her family's mythology, the anointing drew bees to dance around her forehead. Bees have remained a beacon guiding Renée forward as she and her family moved from India to Newfoundland to the Canadian prairies and eventually to Vancouver.

Renée and I have used the library of my 157 scientific publications as field notes to take readers deeper into how research with bees illuminates who we are and who we want to be in the world. We utilized the modes of science and poetry to reflect on what research has taught us about the tension of being an individual living in a society—and about the devastation wrought by our overly intensive management of agricultural and urban habitats.

Listening to the Bees takes readers into the laboratory and out to the field, into the worlds of scientist and beekeepers, and to meetings where the research community intersects with government policy and business. The result is an insiders' view of the way research is conducted—its brilliant potential and its flaws— along with the personal insights and remarkable personalities experienced over a forty-five-year career that parallels the rise of industrial agriculture.

We began our collaboration by performing together at public libraries and beekeeping meetings, reading from my writing interspersed with new poems Renée was creating based on her reading of my scientific papers. As we read, audience members connected to the rhythm of our language and to the stories underlying what bees can teach us. Encouraged by enthusiastic responses, we began writing with a perspective enhanced by our interchange.

We hope this book will similarly engage readers at the juncture of the personal, scientific and poetic, an intersection where research becomes a contemplative adventure to explore the elusive mysteries of who we are and why we are here.

Mark L. Winston
Vancouver, BC

To imagine, sound
To see gesture, the fragment, as series of—
To embed, to crave the sense of the shape of things, the way of—
To write letters, all those un/sent
To trace a pattern, immersed in
To seek erasure, having been—

WHEN READING THE SCIENTIFIC WORK OF MARK AND HIS COLLEAGUES, I enter a state of not-knowing that frees the imagination: poems arrive through a kind of portal, door to a gate, unlocked—arising from, corresponding to, they inhabit their own margins, are constructs, imagined; not literal, they gesture toward—

Everything about this process, of engaging with Mark's scientific work and with his essays in this call-and-response rhythm, produces within me a resonance: to touch the original documents, many of which are at least forty years old, to revel in their construct, the methodology of science and the rhetorical flourishes of its specialized language; to spend time over the names of things, plants and the honeybee—one language leads to another and sometimes, when either reading Mark's work or listening to him, my response emerges in that form in which I practise: embedded fragments and the juxtaposition of opposites, to name a few things in which I delight, fed by curiosity, impressed by the care and attention of these bee scientists. Something about the way things appear on the page, that is the key that unlocks—a kind of finding.

My poetics lean to language as material, and the quest is to marry song, chants, spells and incantations with syntactical wordplay, embroidering the poems I make with numeric patterns, such as my obsession with both hexagons and anything to do with the number six, and the ten-syllable line, whose movement sometimes leads to formal poetic structures such as the sonnet, the villanelle, the madrigal, the sestina and an adaptation of the ghazal where, depending on each form, the stanzas are sometimes revamped to allow lyricism to exist within and alongside the language of science: cribbed, found, merged, less description, more sound and always *the dance most of all.*

Renée Sarojini Saklikar
Vancouver, BC

Mark Winston in French Guiana, 1977, photo by Robin Henschel.

NATURALIST NOTES

THE OLD PHOTO IS MY FAVOURITE, ENCAPSULATING MY SELF-IMAGE AS A naturalist tramping through the South American jungle. I'm standing on a buttress, an enormous above-ground set of roots that provide trees with the additional support they need to keep from falling over in rainforests where the nutrient-poor soil is thin. I'm wearing one of my two sets of khaki clothes, the other in a bucket soaking at home, to be rinsed out and hung to dry overnight to wear tomorrow. The boots are US army jungle surplus, one of the few good things to emerge from the war in Vietnam. The canvas uppers are high and thick enough to protect against snakebites, the leather bottoms sturdy but with ventilation holes to air out the thick tropical humidity.

I'm carrying a leather satchel containing a magnifying glass, collecting vials, and its most important item, my "Naturalist Notes." It was a small, black hardcover journal, not at all distinguished, but it looked to me like something a nineteenth-century British naturalist might carry into the jungle. My inspiration was just such a naturalist, Henry Walter Bates, who wrote the 1863 book *The Naturalist on the River Amazons: a record of the adventures, habits of animals, sketches of Brazilian and Indian life, and aspects of nature under the Equator, during eleven years of travel.*

The Naturalist on the River Amazons documented Bates' expedition to collect species not known to western science, and to provide evidence for the then-newfangled theory of evolution by natural selection. His book was brilliant—a readable and engaging mix of natural history and astute observations about the animals, plants and humans he encountered.

Bates described in compelling detail where and how people lived along the Amazon, what plants and animals they used for food and medicine and how the locals interacted with the Amazon river system and surrounding jungle. He wrote about the exotic plants and animals he encountered, from towering buttressed jungle trees weighed down by vines to the tiniest of beetles and the colourful butterflies from which he developed his classic theories of how and why organisms mimic each other.

I had begun "Naturalist Notes" a few years earlier, while on the scientific version of a vision quest. I was travelling through the Yucatán Peninsula visiting the immensely interesting terrestrial and aquatic ecosystems of that region, hoping to make observations about the natural world that might trigger topics for my graduate research. Copying Bates, I sought clear writing to find that simple formula through which complexity becomes accessible. I wrote about the Yucatán's unusual clear-water mangrove swamps, the interminably deep limestone cenote sinkholes into which the ancient Mayans used to toss their sacrificial victims, the industrious dung beetles who could clean up fresh scat almost before its odour hit the air. My naturalist notes were intertwined with Mayan history, an advanced civilization that precipitously collapsed, leaving behind ruins now largely taken over by jungle. But accents of their former prominence live on in colourful clothing and the Mayan language, still spoken and preferred by many over Spanish.

I held my breath and dove for lobsters off the coast with Mexican fishermen, astounded by how I came up quickly and empty while they stayed down interminably before surfacing with a large Atlantic lobster in each hand. I camped out on beaches or slept in cheap communal hotels, sometimes swinging in brightly coloured Yucatan hammocks large enough to fit entire families. I was writing for myself, but with Bates looking over my shoulder I sought clarity and flow, learning from his example to favour approachable description over jargon. Like Bates, I tried to ask simple questions with broad implications and copied his habit of illustrating with sketches, augmenting my still-forming language with the visual impact of pictures.

I was following the footsteps of Bates, wandering through the tropics until something caught my eye, followed by imposing science onto natural history by posing clear, direct and testable hypotheses. I developed a particular fascination with dung beetles, spending considerable time on my hands and knees observing as they persistently tore off pieces of dung, packed them into tight round balls and rolled them to their nest:

Naturalist Notes: 17 June 1974, Tamazunchale, Mexico

Fascinating low-level cooperation. 2 beetles (seen 3 times), one pointed abdomen and one blunt abdomen (male and female?) roll a round ball of dung three to five times their size downhill. *The male (?) pushes with his hind legs while anchoring his front legs uphill of the dung. The female stands on top of the dung, changing its centre of gravity and aiding the male's pushing. When an obstacle is encountered, the female aids by pulling the dung over the grass, rock or twig. After a few failed attempts, they will change direction. The only directionality consistent was downhill. These creatures raise a number of questions:*

How long-lived is the pair?

Do they build only one burrow?

Do they have a preconceived nest, or just roll until a good site is located?

How far will they roll, and is it always downhill?

Is their motion really random?

How do larvae develop?

Is dung compaction by rolling important?

How does the pair cue itself for cooperation; who tells who which direction, when to push and pull, how hard?

The frustration level of dung beetles!

In hindsight, dung beetles were interesting enough but just a placeholder. I needed a potential project to slot into my applications for a Ph.D. degree, and they would do just fine until something better came along. The tropics, though, were not negotiable. Everything tropical seemed so much more alive than the tamer temperate ecosystems I was familiar with, the wonders of creation more accessible and vibrant. My vision narrowed to an imaginary photo in which I was wearing khaki in a jungle, precise address to be determined.

It would have been a different life, studying dung beetles, but coincidence intervened. I applied to the University of Kansas for graduate school, as they had an excellent history of sending their students travelling to the tropics for their Ph.D. research. Shortly after I was accepted, my supervisor received a large grant to study the African "killer" honeybees that had been accidentally introduced to South America, and that project seemed considerably more adventurous than dung beetles.

As the photograph shows, I did get to actualize that imaginary image in my head into the real thing. What was unexpected, however, was that bees slowly took over my scientific aspirations. I slowly morphed from naturalist to scientist, tropical biology regressing as a target while bee research and beekeeping ascended.

Memory has condensed my affinity for honeybees into that single moment photographed in the jungle, as if an appreciation for the hive downloaded in a millisecond, at first contact. More likely it has been a slow process through many years composed of long hours in innumerable apiaries, and thousands of instances opening up hives, harvesting honey, preparing bees for winter and inspecting colonies in the spring. Interspersed with apiary hours were extended days in pickup trucks driving between apiaries, surrounded by the smells of comb and honey from the back of the truck, punctuated by tramping through fields when the paths in were too muddy, peppered by chats with other beekeepers over coffee and donuts at diners ubiquitous throughout the rural areas where our hives were kept.

All beekeepers are drawn to their bees, but the scientist's focus is further sharpened by applying the rigour of science to the life of the hive. It's a distinctive lens through which to look at bees, the scientific mindset of observing, posing hypotheses, setting up experiments, collecting and analyzing data, seeing patterns, and then asking the next set of questions. What is it about honeybees that make them unusually compelling to study? They are social, for one thing, and social with a complexity that rivals our own. But while complex, honeybee sociality is built from easily observed behaviours, based on decisions that are predictable once observations and experiments have elucidated their patterns.

Our human behaviours are not as easily categorized, possibly because the underlying rules that guide our decisions are not as simple, or perhaps we are just too close to our own species to accurately discern our own behaviours. And, bees can be experimentally manipulated, with thousands of individuals as potential data points in even a single hive. Manipulating humans is both unethical and impractical; the most fundamental tool of science, experiments, is off limits to researchers.

Still, the social mechanisms that contribute to smooth colony functioning in bees are not very different from those we depend on in our human societies.

There are many lessons we can learn from observing how bees blend many individuals into a community. Colony success depends on constant and open communication, a flexible workforce, collaborative decision-making and putting the communal good above that of the individual. These social elements are all integral to how well our human communities function, or don't.

Studying honeybees is also compelling because of their obvious reliance on nature, an element of human existence we too often lose sight of. It's pretty simple for bees: virtually all their food comes from floral nectar and pollen produced by plants to attract bees to pollinate. Neither bees nor many plants would exist without this healthy codependency. It's just as simple for us but less obvious through our actions, given the harmful ways we continue to disrupt the very environment we depend on.

Studying bees is attractive for another reason: bee research yields practical benefits for honey production and pollination, in addition to the awe that emerges from studies of their basic biology. Almost any topic of fundamental biological interest also has concrete economic ramifications, so that basic and applied science are virtually seamless when bees are the study organism.

Doing science with bees as my escort also yielded unexpected personal benefits. Here again memory serves me poorly, but I suspect I was as shallow and self-absorbed as most young adults. But bees provided a different model for how to be in the world: collaborative and communicative, listening deeply to others, being present in the moment. Over time I came to prefer communal interests to solitary pursuits, absorbing the ethic of the hive as my spirit guide.

I did get to inhabit that vision of myself as tropical biologist, but my totemic photograph did not turn out to be the end point. Rather, the tropics' lure was subsumed by the enticements of the hive, and by the practical consideration of a job in Canada and a young family. Instead of wandering through the tropics using science to uncover nature's compelling revelations, I learned to roam deeply into bee colonies, imposing science onto natural history by posing clear, direct and testable hypotheses.

Bees provide the same mystical element that had attracted me to the tropics, the miracles of creation and evolution, nature and science, intertwining right there every time you crack the lid of the hive.

THOSE OLD PHOTOGRAPHS

un

rivers searched, calling
feral, boxed, stripped wax

after the hive
had been searched
the frames were
examined again
and replaced,
      in their original order

deux

those prisoners, named
ghosts, that town, settled, the past—
five colonies, hived

trois

swarm to swarm, those bees
suspended, their own comb built
top-bars, wood moving

after hiving, at five-day intervals
inspections continued
until no marked bees were present

quatre

the sixth colony
glass walls, a two-frame hive

one thousand bees
each cohort
an equivalent

cinq

and sat cross-legged
chanting, come we, come *oui,* who—

causative factors
age-specific probabilities
            and shift

six

    and we, being ghosts
        could not hold onto—

Mark Winston in the Lynn Margulis laboratory, about 1971, photographer unknown.

A FIFTY-MILLION-YEAR-OLD SKULL

My path to bees and science did not begin in the jungles, but rather with some latex and a fifty-million-year-old fossil skull from Wyoming that provided my first exposure to research. The skull's discoverer was Leonard Radinsky, a paleontology professor at the University of Chicago, where I spent two years as an undergraduate student beginning in 1968.

It was a curious choice to spend most of my freshman year carefully scraping the sand and dirt from a fossil skull rather than attend classes. The University of Chicago was and still is considered one of the world's most distinguished universities, renowned for its "Life of the Mind" curriculum, exposing students to the entire history of human thought in science, arts, literature, history and politics.

While the university attempted to immerse us in the great minds, the city outside was close to a state of war, convulsed with protests against the war in Vietnam, recent police brutality at the Democratic National Convention, and the horrific poverty and crime spilling over from the adjacent black ghetto on the south side of Chicago. Lingering outside these two disconnected worlds of town and gown was a compelling personal reality: I needed to earn some money if I was to stay in school and maintain my student exemption from the US military draft, which loomed as a heavy consequence of dropping out. My salvation came in the form of an advertisement for a research assistant in the Department of Anatomy. Professor Radinsky was seeking an undergraduate student to assist in a project studying brain evolution in carnivores. I had no interest in brains, or carnivores, but it was a job and since I was the only applicant, my lack of experience or any interest in the field were not barriers.

His project involved a narrow, highly academic topic of interest to but a few specialists, and no apparent relevance to the street protests that were engaging most of my enthusiasm. Radinsky studied the Tertiary Period, especially forty-five-to-fifty-six-million-year-old fossils from Wyoming, a time and place when the ancestors of current carnivores thrived while other then-populous lines of carnivores declined and disappeared. His window into the information retained in fossils was to pour liquid latex into ancient skulls to create casts. He then examined the impressions on the solidified latex to deduce the size and fold structures of the long-ago brains. His work tested a theory rampaging at the time through the tiny community of brain paleontologists—that successful carnivores evolved larger brains and essentially out-thought the evolutionary losers.

My first fossil to clean and cast was from a line of carnivores that didn't make it out of the Tertiary. Radinsky handed it to me casually with no apparent concern that I would fumble and destroy this irreplaceable relic from an extraordinarily distant past. He clearly put a higher priority on my learning than he did on the history that I might destroy in the process. It didn't look like much, covered by a concretion of sand and pebbles. I gingerly began to chip away and reveal the fossil within, feeling a responsibility for preserving the information embedded in the skull. My focus and interest was enhanced by the real consequences if my hand slipped or my attention wandered, infused with that sense of wonder and engagement that had eluded me in the classroom.

Slowly the fossil emerged, after many weeks of meticulously slow and painstaking work, until I could pour in the latex and pop out the cast holding impressions made by the brain on its surrounding skull. It was a poignant moment, seeing the folds and valleys of an animal that not only was long dead itself, but whose descendants had gone extinct through the crucible of natural selection. It was also a personal eureka moment, my first taste of how systematic, rigorous probing through science could reveal the secrets of ancient, now-extinct organisms, opening for us a window into how we evolved and our position in the contemporary world. The secret revealed through this study was that the big brain hypothesis was incorrect, and in fact successful carnivores had brains no larger than those who disappeared from the evolutionary tree.

I transferred to Boston University in 1970, mostly to be with my then-girlfriend, and there I continued to be a seriously underperforming undergraduate student bored by classes and distracted by, well, all the things that distract a young man of twenty. But I still needed a job, and after my Chicago experience I had a template for how research could be a painless pathway to earn money while at university. I began knocking on faculty doors to see if I could find a research position while displaying my usual outfit of overalls, long, unkempt hair and beard, and a pathetic transcript loaded with Cs and Ds. After being quickly refused and dismissed at every door, I finally found myself at Lynn Margulis's office door.

I had no idea that Lynn was among the most stellar evolutionary biologists of the last one hundred years, and Boston University's most famous scientist at the time. To me, she was just another door to knock on and face what I had come to expect as inevitable rejection. But instead, she dragged me into her office and spent most of that afternoon passionately and enthusiastically introducing me to primitive one-celled organisms. She pulled out old articles by Harvard professor L.R. Cleveland, and the work of obscure Russian protozoologists, about the magnificent symbiotic organisms that live in termite guts. I understood little of what she was saying, but was hooked by her passion. To my great surprise she gave me a summer job, and let me loose in her lab to do real research.

In spite of her stratospheric accomplishments and reputation, Lynn had little in the way of grant money, due to her reputation as a maverick and an outspoken critic of how mainstream science was funded and conducted. Being a strong-minded woman in 1970s science, with what were then radical scientific ideas, was not endearing to granting bodies. But oddly she did have some funds to develop a new screening method for anti-cancer drugs. The idea was to examine how the potential drugs interfered with the growth of tiny hairs (cilia) that make up the mouthparts of one-celled organisms. These hairs are made of the same proteins that create the push-and-pull structures that divide cells. If a drug interfered with the mouthpart hairs, it might also interfere with the out-of-control cell division that characterizes cancer.

My first task was to do a twenty-four-hour experiment in which I shocked the cilia to shed with chemicals, then followed their regeneration every two hours in the presence of various doses of potential anti-cancer drugs. Control cells would take about eight hours to regenerate, and our hope was that the anti-cancer drugs would slow or prevent regeneration until at least the next day.

I began at eight a.m., checking the dishes of pond water in which the cells were swimming every two hours, recording the state of the hairs. It got to be dinnertime, then later, and it occurred to me that I would be up all night with this experiment doing my two-hour checks. Fortunately, I had friends in the neighbourhood near the laboratory who habitually stayed up late imbibing various things and partying. I joined in, but returned to the lab faithfully every two hours to collect the data.

By the next morning I was overtired and in a somewhat altered state, but dying to know whether the results meant anything. After the last eight a.m. check, I took out a piece of graph paper and recorded each two-hour data point. To my amazement the data formed a perfect straight line; the dose of drug was exactly related to how long it took the cilia to regenerate.

A perfect fit. Exactly related. Unusual in science, but a life changer for me. Through these early experiences I realized that a well-conceived experiment could reveal something about the world no one had known before, peeling off the tiniest, tiniest sliver from the unknown.

THE LEGEND OF THE BEES

lotus petals folded open, floating—
that name forgotten, servant girl dancing
warmed copper pot, a drop of oil swirled, poured
those shadow puppets, papery thin, cut
stingless *Trigona*—*Bauhinia* tree
planted earthenware and enormous, above
the bees, hind legs bundled with white pollen
baby, red Paithani saree wrapped, un-
tied, ankles released, brown eyes ready to
focus, that threshold, long beans after flowers
hollowed, dry stem above the trunk, that's how
they'd get in, to nest, and then would fly out
circling above, forehead untouched, sweet
emanations just beyond reach, endless—

Mistress tree—
    Mahalakshmi root,
        from your branches, your Shiva arms

they will come in hundreds, thousands, wrapped—
    filial(s) of grey moss (hidden) jewels.

Mother-Father tree, displaying *alkīmiyā* alchemy:
water, light, air.   At your command, roots
    run sap.

Come wind, the rain. A tree-clock teleology
    propels time forward.
Almost.

The way you work, bit by bit, covert,
    infinitesimal green
        a dance,
 anima, animus,   embrace of branches from your helix spine
        eight, ten, twelve tributaries
        a swerve and the tallest curve

each day   the space   between your branches, fills.
Quiet.   Change drops in stealth:

buds push out from grooves, sprockets,
    the tuber-heads on your arms.
how sly you are, all around rising with the sun,
    a dance and hum
    we, devotees—

they told a family story
round that fire long ago,

in that country, dreams rose, misty—
mountains, terraced hills, Shiva, a waterfall

that last time—down by the river Krishna
or higher up and away

tin-roofed bungalow
white khadi sheets, to swaddle:

baby girl lying on a saree-blanket
lotus flowers   daybreak—
            those swarming bees, only a handful remained
            enough to encircle her

One-room schoolhouse, Lawrence, Kansas, photo from map data@2017 Google.

THE ONE-ROOM SCHOOLHOUSE

IT WAS A RED BRICK FORMER ONE-ROOM SCHOOLHOUSE, STANDING FOR-lorn and isolated at the edge of a swatch of Midwestern prairie. I was similarly lonely, having just arrived in Lawrence, Kansas to take up graduate studies with no place to live, very little money and no job to support myself. That August was particularly hot and humid, even for a Kansas summer, quite a comedown from the Cape Cod sea breezes, salt marshes, sand dunes and ocean vistas I had left behind just as few days before. I had abandoned many friends, a developing career in marine biology and a classically quaint Cape-style cottage to pursue a different life, that of an entomologist studying bees.

It was a desolate moment, that arrival, but good fortune soon shifted my mood. Within hours I checked in at the entomology department, and a few min-utes later the sympathetic chair of the department provided me with both a job and a free place to live. The job was bread-and-butter graduate student employ-ment, working as a teaching assistant in a biology class, but the living arrange-ments were, well, unusual.

I headed out that afternoon to the edge of the city to take up my new residence, a former schoolhouse that had been taken over by the entomology department and nicknamed the "bee house," a research facility used to study bees and wasps. All I had to do in return for a bed, a hot plate, a small refrigerator, worn wooden floors and blackboarded walls was inhabit the place to discourage vandals.

There were a few disadvantages the chair hadn't mentioned. For one, I couldn't open the windows, in spite of the daily 100° F temperatures, because each window had a papery grey wasp nest hung on the outside, study colonies for a graduate student interested in how wasps organized their social behaviour. Lack of privacy was another trade-off for no rent, with students coming in at all hours of the day and night, not only to record behaviours from the window nests but also to traipse around the basement, which was full of more wasp nests as well as colonies of halictid bees that nested in dirt. The wasp-studying students were having an art contest, putting coloured paper into Plexiglas boxes for the wasps to use as building material, creating rainbow nests. The bee guys had taken a layer of dirt one bee width in diameter and sandwiched it between two sheets of plate glass, so that they could observe the bee behaviours.

Weekdays and many weekends I spent up the hill on campus, taking classes, reading journal articles, writing research proposals for funding, going to seminars and teaching undergraduate laboratories. Evenings I was alone, and after my hot-plate dinners I often descended to the bee house basement for hymenopteran company, mesmerized watching the wasps build their nests of many colours and the bees bumping into each other as they navigated the tunnels they had carved into the dirt.

Graduate school is like that, lonely at first, an unbalanced experience with work predominant and social life suppressed. But as the bee and wasp nests died off and fall arrived, I physically and metaphorically opened the windows. My evenings soon filled with friends, guitar playing, and student potluck dinners followed by dancing to country swing music at local clubs. Midnight often found us at the *Rocky Horror Picture Show*, and we met many a dawn at Jennings Daylight Donuts.

I also soon had a different job, a research assistantship spent looking through a microscope for hours drawing bee mouthparts. The work provided the income I needed to go to South America for a year, to study killer bees in French Guiana for my doctoral degree. Even while away I thought of the bee house as home, and felt cruelly uprooted when I returned to Lawrence a year later to find the schoolhouse no longer mine, taken over by the next impoverished graduate student who had arrived in my absence. Now I had to live like a regular person, renting an apartment with rooms and a real kitchen and no bees or wasps as co-tenants.

But perhaps my year in the bee house had primed me for a different way to think about the meaning of home. Living in the schoolhouse, I imprinted on the company of bees and wasps. Every new dwelling since has not become home until I connect with the local social insects. I've put a honeybee colony into the backyard, valued the wasp nest growing under the eaves, enjoyed the mating ants flying up from beneath the sidewalk, bonded with the neighbourhood bees foraging on my lawn and garden, and even appreciated the termites gnawing at the foundations of our fixer-upper starter home. A journalist asked me once to describe my first visit to a honeybee hive, and my response was that "I opened the lid of that first hive, began pulling out combs of bees, and I felt like I was home." Home is where the heart is, and my heart, still, is with the bees.

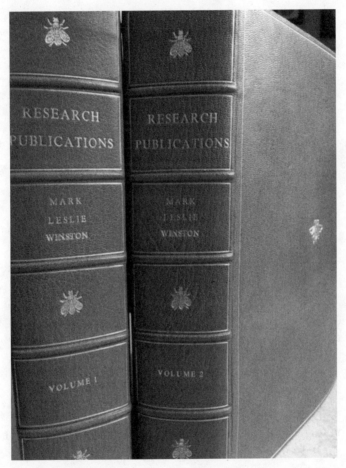

Full bound set of Mark Winston research publications, photo by Mark Winston.

Drawing of fossil Halictid bee, lower Eocene, courtesy of Bruce Archibald.

EMBEDDED AND SET

that photograph, framed

that fault-bounded montane, basin where
      clastic, derived from volcanic

sand-scraped, shaken, brushed
      sandstones in the cold-water beds

granitic rocks, paleocurrents
      conglomerate, sandstones and coal

eocene: on zircons extracted, with the shales

an old road cut—exposure
           southward-dipping

light buff to dark brown

mudstones, fissile shales, volcanic tuff
      those found, carbonaceous, compressions

the part, corresponding

impressions, counter
      as—those lines traced—

Hymenoptera

ancient lake, whose beds
and we, with herbal salves, lip balms

honey and vinegar—
no memory, a memory: conifer resin

to trap, hold
that pattern

delicate, ancient
eocene—

that series, freshwater
driftwood, horsefly

said soft on the tongue

derived from

and searched, generations, documents
        dust covered, those riverbeds
           that ghost lineage

lakebed shale, terrestrial
        where flowers were—
           fresh volcanic ash

one fossil to another

that lost tribe, *Electrapini*
            female worker
                        poor and preserved
            wings outstretched
ventral portions   incomplete

at the surface of the amber—
body of the holotype

Melikertes
            (Paremelikertes)
gujaratensis

simple setae
branched

a genus of
and extinct

many
small
veins
arising

camera lucida

        thin layers
    those specimens
            circular parts
                distilled

                o sing to us, they said

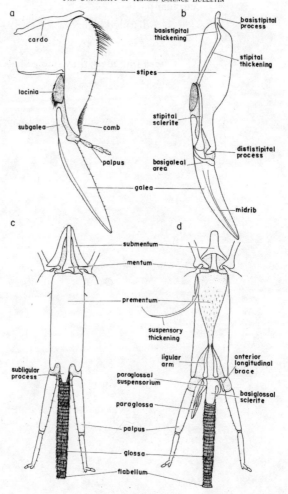

Fig. 2: Representative views of generalized labiomaxillary complex, showing nomenclature of structures. a) outer view of the maxilla, b) inner view of the maxilla, c) posterior view of the labium, d) anterior view of the labium.

University of Kansas Science Bulletin, 1979, drawing by Mark Winston.

MOUTHPARTS OF
THE LONG-TONGUED BEES

AT ONE POINT EARLY IN MY CAREER I WAS RECOGNIZED AS THE WORLD'S expert in the labiomaxillary complex of the long-tongued bees, at least among the half-dozen or so entomologists for whom bee mouthparts mattered. I achieved this obscure recognition as a graduate student at the University of Kansas by dissecting, drawing and analyzing mouthparts from about one hundred species across the thousands that make up this diverse bee group. The other bees have short tongues and were studied by another student, who ascended to the short-tongued throne. Tongue length makes a difference to bees, as it determines what flowers they can collect nectar from.

Admittedly obscure, this study nevertheless transformed my scientific career, not so much for the scientific findings as for the cultural lessons I learned from my mentor in the project, the eminent bee biologist Charles Michener. Mich was a prodigy, publishing his first paper on bees when he was sixteen and going on to reach the highest levels of academia. In 1948, he had published a paper describing the evolutionary relationships between all bees, a monumental achievement that formed the bible of bee taxonomy for decades.

What changed everything for me was the basistipital process, a tiny obscure protuberance found on some long-tongued mouthparts but not on others. What made this structure important was that it differed in the highly social honeybees and stingless bees. Tracing its evolution back through more primitive bees suggested that each group had evolved social behaviour independently. If so, this was a career-building discovery, as the evolution of complex social behaviour is rare. The key implication of this finding was that sociality had evolved not once but twice among the bees. Studies of insect social behaviour were and still are important areas of research, in part because we too are a highly social species and can learn much about our own evolution and behaviour by examining that of the bees.

I quickly realized the important implications of the basistipital process, but my next thought was more terror than exhilaration. If I was right, then Mich's classic study was incorrect. I would have to tell one of the greatest biologists of our time that he was wrong. It was with considerable trepidation, and after much procrastination, that I made an appointment to see Mich and brought him my findings. I was well prepared with specimens and my arguments, but was surprised by his reaction.

Mich was fascinated rather than defensive. Without the slightest sign of disappointment, he said we needed to reexamine the honeybees and stingless bees to see if other evidence would challenge his 1948 conclusions. We went on to look at other structures, particularly those on the legs used to collect pollen, and a wide range of social behaviours in the two groups. The evidence was strong, and we published a paper in the prestigious *Proceedings of the US National Academy of Science* (*PNAS*) proposing the dual origin of highly social behaviour among the bees.

I'm a big appreciator of how moments in life can have lasting impact. That appointment with Mich was one of those moments for me, when he was open to contradicting his own classic and much-cited work if the evidence supported it. He modelled for me how science is not a right or wrong polarity but a continually evolving examination of new data. When the data contradict the theory, it's appropriate to dump even the most hallowed hypothesis. I also learned from Mich to appreciate those moments of surprise in science when the evidence suggests the hypothesis you have based years of work on is wrong. My own students have been startled expecting me to be disappointed when their experiments don't prove my pet theory to be correct, and I treat their negative data as a eureka moment. It's in the negative results that progress in science is born.

I learned one more lesson from Mich through the humble basistipital process. He let me write and be the first author on the *PNAS* paper, even though this was an important publication, I was an obscure student and he was, well, the Great One in bees. I still choke up recalling this incredible kindness, and hope I have emulated his generosity with my own students.

And there is a postscript: about ten years later new molecular techniques became available that allowed comparisons of proteins and even genes between groups of organisms. When applied to the long-tongued bees, the results suggested that Michener's original taxonomy was correct, and our dual origin proposal perhaps was not accurate. It remains an ongoing issue in social insect biology, still with no definitive conclusion.

SAID THE BEEKEEPER

a nest, papery grey
tucked string, unknotted

come the spring
we'd braid strands

pulp fibres
wind wisps caught

layers stuck
tissue thin

six-sided
scrape scrape scrape

saliva, that slow descent
her jaws and open
we sprayed her
      that aerosol foam
           morning
                at first light

LABIOMAXILLARY

i.

dis-
tis-
ti-
pi-
tal.

ii.

an-
ter-
ior.

iii.

basi-
glossal.

iv.

galea

v.

we'd not seen any—

vi.

lost.

(PARAMELIKERTES) GUJARATENSIS

parched   lips   parse   words   grit laden soil on soil
bats   swipe at the gloaming   soft light's tendril

fingers curl   evening's blue hours   grass threads hands
nails splinter   in a gust of air—dusk's tendrils

one candle singes   midnight and this pencil wavers
minute to minute ash burns   wisps   wax tendrils

this stolen form lingers   Farsi lingers Urdu lingers Gujarati lingers
Boreas north wind   speak of such things as life's tendrils

Beloved this night of dust turns earth's tumbrel turns papery with longing
wine spills on sand   moonlight sears   time's tendrils

earth eats moonlight   roses   black tips red on dung four pellets of goose droppings
two winds two limbs   N'aschi   Shamal   breath tendrils

a great longing for sleep surges into twilight's dirge
azure night   a shawl   silk's unravelling tendrils

nose to find a scent   spectacles to magnify a tear
mouth to mouth the long drape of death's tendrils

beloved   your name rises in the east   dawn's sifted syllables
aurora sings shadows drift over stone   [   ] tendrils

STINGLESS BEES

THE NETFLIX TELEVISION SERIES *STRANGER THINGS* DEPICTS AN ALTERNATE universe, one of many existing side-by-side with our own. A passage opens between one of those realities and ours due to a bizarre mind-training experiment perpetrated on a young girl by a top-secret wing of the US government, and it wouldn't be revealing any spoilers to tell you that some serious fright results. The mind-manipulated girl comes up with distinctive language to describe the other reality, calling it the "upside-down world." It's like a flipped version of our own, where things are familiar but nothing seems quite right.

I think of stingless bees that way, as honeybee's upside-down counterpart. Honeybees were my entry point into the world of social insects, so I imprinted on their behaviour and social culture as normal. My encounters with stingless bees came later and seemed like a warped version of social insect reality, disconcerting by being simultaneously familiar yet foreign.

"Stingless" for a bee may seem like a contradiction, since stinging is one of the traits we associate with bees, but this group of highly social bees is not at all defenseless. The five hundred or so species of stingless bees have lost their sting but in its place have evolved wicked bites, often accompanied by blister-inducing venom, that are highly effective at driving off marauders.

My first close look at stingless bees happened in French Guiana on the northeast coast of South America, and involved some close observations of bees collecting pollen on flowers. French Guiana itself is an upside-down place, replete with contradictions. It's a protectorate of France, with feral jungle and coastal savannahs adjacent to the Guiana Space Centre used by the European Space Agency and France's National Centre for Space Studies. A typical Guyanese restaurant might serve jungle meat such as jaguar, anaconda, capybara and even monkey brains, with a side order of fresh baguette flown in on daily nonstop flights from Paris.

I was there studying the African "killer" bees that were moving northward from Brazil and colonizing French Guiana when we arrived in 1976. As a side project, I was also looking at the anatomy of bee mouthparts. A few structures suggested that the stingless bees and the honeybees, although both highly social, might have evolved separately, and represented two pinnacles of social evolution rather than evolving from a common social ancestor.

There were abundant stingless bees from diverse species collecting pollen from flowers in French Guiana, so my colleagues and I decided to examine how they manipulated pollen and compare that specific behaviour with pollen handling by honeybees. The most defining characteristic of bees is that they have plumose hairs with which they groom pollen from flowers and pack it onto specialized structures on their legs or abdomens to carry this protein-rich food back to their nests. Thus, how bees manipulate pollen has been of great interest to entomologists as a tool to probe the evolution and taxonomic relationships of bees.

It's the packing process that turned out to be upside-down for stingless bees and honeybees. Honeybees groom pollen from one side of their body and transfer it to the basket on the opposite hind leg, while the stingless bees groom pollen and pack it into the basket on the same side leg. That may seem like a small difference, and alone wouldn't be much to draw conclusions from. But the combination of differing mouthpart anatomy and pollen manipulation behaviours was enough to inspire a closer look at other traits. We began accumulating a compelling list of characteristics that disagreed between the stingless and the honeybees, evidence that they were indeed upside-down versions of each other.

Stinglessness was a particularly disquieting trait differentiating the two groups. We chopped down and cut open palm trees and other small trees to study honeybee nests, and a stingless bee colony would often reside in the same tree. Both species would be furious at our incursion. Being attacked simultaneously by the stinging end of honeybees and the biting end of stingless bees is unsettling, viscerally emphasizing that these two groups of bees inhabit parallel spheres, similar yet different.

Numerous other characteristics indicate how the stingless bees and honeybees live in corresponding realities. Both reproduce by swarming, where some of the workers from the old colony leave the nest and find a new one. In honeybees, the old queen leaves the nest with workers, clustering together underneath a branch or other overhang. The swarm sends out scouts, finds a new site, flies to it and then the workers begin secreting wax and building comb. In the stingless bees, scouts from the old nest first find a new nest. Then, some of the workers take wax from the old colony and use it to construct the new home. When the new domicile is ready, the original colony rears a new queen who leaves with some of the workers and flies directly to the new site without clustering first.

Honeybees and stingless bees also differ in how they attract workers from their nests to flowers. Stingless bees buzz nestmates in the nest and then lead them to flowers, sometimes also setting down an odour trail to the floral resources. Honeybees have evolved a complex dance language that represents the location of flowers abstractly, but accurately enough that naïve foragers can follow the dance in the nest and then find the flowers on their own, without being led or following an odour trail.

Many other differences emerged from our study, involving varied styles of nest building, different timing for when and how much to feed larvae, and anatomical differences including where wax-producing glands are located on the workers and the shape of the cells that make up comb. Beyond the details, here's what was clear at the end of our study: both groups of bees are highly social but evolved to solve similar problems through behaviours and structures evocative of but not identical to each other.

Each inhabits what a sci-fi aficionado might imagine as the upside-down world of the other, but we don't need to evoke the upside-down to appreciate how evolutionary problem-solving in our own singularity can lead to distinctive responses to the same selection pressures. We biologists call it convergence: *organisms not closely related independently evolve similar traits as a result of having to adapt to similar environments or ecological niches.*

Perhaps the most well-known convergence is that of bats, birds and flying fish, all taxonomically distant but all having wings that evolved independently of the others. Similarly, bats and whales orient using high-frequency echolocation, one while flying through the air and the other underwater, again with no close evolutionary connection between them. Baleen whales and basking sharks have comparable filter-feeding structures to consume plankton, but one's a mammal and the other a primitive fish. My personal favourite convergence is between koala bears and humans. Distant on the taxonomic tree, we're identical in one trait: koalas have fingerprints that are indistinguishable from human. Fingerprints enhance the sense of touch that is critical for the fine motor skill necessary to grasp objects, a behaviour that koalas and we excel in. If I were a crime novelist, I'd certainly take advantage of this eerie convergence.

The evolutionary convergence of stingless bees and honeybees is a reminder that what we consider upside down in nature depends on what's recognizable. The Mayans who maintained colonies of stingless bees in Central America for honey would have been shocked to see the first introduced honeybees, clearly foreign yet in their convergence with stingless bees vaguely familiar. In North America honeybees were called "the white man's fly" by indigenous tribes, who discovered quickly that the arrival of wild swarms preceded the waves of settlers moving west that decimated native populations.

It's not necessary to invoke parallel universes to appreciate that even in our own universe there are versions of reality unique to each of our experiences and sensibilities. Nature can perform the same function for us as science fiction: a way in to appreciate the splendid diversity of alternative universes that make up the singular space and time we inhabit.

TORN FROM THE BOOK OF
THE GREAT GATHERING

th   at   fam-   ily Halictidae

        work- ed

catmint clover dogwood sunflower—

verbena-

                sa   lt se   ek   ers,

met allic

shak-

en, dau

                gh ters to re-
                main,
                        nest
ed flat,
close-
groun-   ded,   cell s   wat-

er-
proofed, waxed.

ALL ALONG THAT HEDGEROW

chokecherry-wildflower-meadow-birch-corn
       hawthorn-gooseberry-red-osier-dogwood
that shape, those cells, cylindrical at first
       isodiametric and arranged, tight
pussy willow-snowberry-sunflowers
crimson clover-yarrow-balsam poplar

pussy willow-snowberry-sunflowers
       crimson clover-yarrow-balsam poplar
that shape, those cells, cylindrical at first
       isodiametric and arranged, tight
hawthorn-gooseberry-red-osier-dogwood
chokecherry-wildflower-meadow-birch-corn

crimson clover-yarrow-balsam poplar
       pussy willow-snowberry-sunflowers
isodiametric and arranged, tight
       that shape, those cells, cylindrical at first
chokecherry-wildflower-meadow-birch-corn
hawthorn-gooseberry-red-osier-dogwood

hawthorn-gooseberry-red-osier-dogwood
    chokecherry-wildflower-meadow-birch-corn
that shape, those cells, cylindrical at first
    isodiametric and arranged, tight
pussy willow-snowberry-sunflowers
crimson clover-yarrow-balsam poplar

dogwood-osier-red-gooseberry-hawthorn
    corn-birch-meadow-wildflower-chokecherry
isodiametric and arranged, tight
    that shape, those cells, cylindrical at first
pussy willow-snowberry-sunflowers
crimson clover-yarrow-balsam poplar

chokecherry-wildflower-meadow-birch-corn
    hawthorn-gooseberry-red-osier-dogwood
that shape, those cells, cylindrical at first
    isodiametric and arranged, tight
pussy willow-snowberry-sunflowers
crimson clover-yarrow-balsam poplar—

CROSS-FOSTERED

OUR KILLER BEE TEAM WAS FOLLOWING THE AFRICAN BEES' COLONIZING front as part of our research strategy. In 1978, we moved our base of operations from French Guiana northwest along the South American coast to the small town of Laguna Grande outside of Maturin, Venezuela, to be closer to where swarms were beginning to arrive in large numbers.

We seemed fated to locate near prisons. In French Guiana, we could see the infamous Devil's Island penal colony offshore from some of our apiaries. Maturin was an affluent centre for Venezuela's oil industry, but the village near Laguna Grande where we were located was anything but prosperous. It's best described as a collection of shacks and shanties that had sprung up around a prison, with most of the town's residents either working for or having family members in the local jail.

We were in Maturin by invitation of the Venezuelan government, as part of a substantial aid project to support beekeepers as the African bees moved into the country. The Ministry of Agriculture's concern for beekeeping and the public was justified; four hundred people were stung to death the year we arrived, and beekeepers were having a hard time finding sites to keep their hives. The government agreed to build us a field station where we could live and work in return for research useful to the local beekeepers.

The field station and the fate of the project were instructive in revealing the tragic underbelly of Venezuela's ineffective and corrupt government. The station itself was a cinder block facility with cooking/living space as well as a research laboratory, located within a mango plantation that supplied us with more fruit than we could possibly consume in a lifetime. The station was equipped with everything the Venezuelan government imagined we North Americans would need, from air conditioners to waffle irons to indoor plumbing to a guard to protect us at night. But the electricity rarely worked and if we flushed the toilets we'd find the contents floating up into the showers. The guard, Ramon, we'd find passed out inebriated every morning in our driveway.

The aid portion of the project was equally problematic. The US government had funded the purchase of a considerable quantity of beekeeping equipment and non-African queens to distribute to local beekeepers, most of whom had little training and operated only a small number of colonies each. The equipment and queens soon vanished, however, and we eventually learned they had been siphoned off into the commercial beekeeping operation of someone high up in the Venezuelan Ministry of Agriculture. Still, we managed to conduct a fair bit of research, including what turned out to be a fascinating project revealing the basis for many of the African bees' problematic behaviours, and also addressing the key issue of whether there was any way to stop the bees before they arrived in North America.

In one set of experiments we borrowed a research tool from the discipline of psychology, cross-fostering. It compares attributes of individuals raised in parental environments to those raised in foreign situations, which allows researchers to tease out the relative importance of genetics and environment. We cross-fostered newly emerged and marked adult worker bees from two honey-bee subspecies, those from a tropical African background and those from more temperate European climates, by introducing them into colonies of their own race and colonies of the other race. Thus, there were four groups: European bees in European colonies, European bees in African colonies, African bees in African colonies and African bees in European colonies.

We removed frames from colonies that had young bees emerging, called by the delightful entomological term "teneral," meaning soft and immature. Tenerals less than a day old, before their cuticle had hardened, are too young to sting and are easily handled. We labelled each bee with a coloured and numbered tag glued to their backs, and reintroduced them to either their own colony or a colony from the other race. Our objective was to compare two characteristics that might have both a genetic and an environmental component: the ages at which worker bees began foraging and their lifespans. These traits are related, since foraging workers are exposed to many more mortality threats than those in the hive.

Each day we went out to the apiaries and sat in front of colonies midday when the bees were foraging, recording the identity of each bee we saw leaving or returning to the nest. This was a bit more dangerous than it might appear, and not because of the bees. Mangos would periodically drop on us from the orchard where our research hives were located, as would the occasional snake, but since our observation times were carefully timed we couldn't move until the study session was over. We also went through the hives once a week, early in the morning before any bees left to forage. One of us would take frames out one by one and announce the identity of each bee we saw: Yellow 51, Blue 26, and so on. The other would record who was still alive into the small waterproof Clairefontaine notebook that we favoured for data collection.

The results indicated an interaction between genetics and environment. In their own colonies, African workers foraged earlier and died younger, whereas European workers in their own colonies foraged later and lived longer. However, when cross-fostered the African worker bees became more like the Europeans, foraging at about the same age as the European bees and living similar lifespans. The European bees in African colonies became even more African than the Africans, foraging at even younger ages and living considerably shorter lives.

Basically, European bees live a slower and less frenetic life in their own hives, while the African bees in their own colonies are wired, living faster and dying younger. But put the Africans into a European colony and they slow down, whereas the Europeans in an African colony live faster and die even younger than their host African bees. Thus, while both genetics and environment were important, colony environment trumped genetic background, so that nurture dominated nature.

The idea of a barrier zone across Mexico had been floated to stop the northward spread of the African bees, with tens of thousands of European colonies providing drones that would mate with the wild African queens and genetically swamp the African traits. Our results indicated that not only did the African bees have a genetic disposition to the fast and furious, but hybrid bees in colonies with African queens that had mated with European drones (males) would behave even more like African bees than the Africans themselves. Thus, a genetic barrier to the African spread would be ineffective. This didn't stop the US Department of Agriculture from investing over $10 million in just such a zone. Not surprisingly, it was a dismal failure, as the African bees moved through the zone genetically intact, with colony traits possibly even worsened by the presence of some mixed-race hybrid bees through mating.

The issue of genetics vs. environment, nature or nurture, is much easier to approach in an animal model than in human society, where the personal and social implications are considerably more difficult to untangle. Arguments quickly polarize towards choosing nurture or nature, and both extremes have been used to justify social policy. At times our perspective has been that we humans can overcome our genetic background if only we try hard enough. At other times, we support the idea that genetics is destiny. Our experimental results provide compelling evidence that behavioural traits involve an interaction between genetics and environment. The African and European bees were indeed different in their home environments, but when removed and placed in a different home they would adopt the qualities expressed by their new family. DNA matters, but life experience matters as much or more.

The words "nature" and "nurture" are most often used in opposition: nature *or* nurture. But it would be more accurate to say "nature *and* nurture," recognizing that genetics and environment form an interaction, not a polarization, and together lead to identity. That's heartening for our human condition, because it allows for the possibility of choice while recognizing that our complex genetic ancestors also contribute to who we are. Human tenerals may have some hardwired traits, but like the bees our human young can be influenced for better or worse by home and community.

Swarm of Africanized bees, with Chip Taylor from the University of Kansas, 1976, photo by Mark Winston.

LINES OF DESCENT

Bombini, Apini, Meliponini
          they took scraps of paper
                    torn from a thousand books
here was printed:
          stingless bees, pollen from the middle leg
a curvature—into the corbicula—

Submentum, they would whisper at night
          unaware of each other
Trigona, three syllables to cherish

winged, ventilated, stingless—
          this was the night-saying, recited around fires
a transference:

the workings of bees, pollen
          front legs, the middle—
stingless, primitive, imagined.

They recited without understanding
          loving the words:
soft wax, resin, torn down after
                    a single use.

DANCE OF THE BEES IN THE COURT
OF THE QUEEN OF SEASONS

Of her flourishing waltzes,
        brocaded with flower,
many will sing.
        Seeded with petal bunches—ruffed collar,
her petticoats, flowers,
and upwards, some will look to the sky.

Her trunk will hide mountains, rivers, an entire city,
dressed by peaks, valley of a dazzling white
            this flower-fabric, an ocean,
the tree, a galleon, a waterfall, cascading into air.

Her dance will ride morning's partner,
        paltry asphalt—cement corner block, such meagre admirers
            overcome by grandiosity; it does not matter.
Everyone, courtier: bridges, buses, a van full of children,
            woman in a high tower, tiny speck
                unnoticed but still bowing.

Even the trains down by the river call out their sigh-song
        otherworldly shunting no match for blossom splendour.
Somewhere, on a telephone wire,
        a robin sings to the beat of the tree's stationary dance:
            full flower song.

By afternoon, hours heavy with petal, she usurps her own season,
       is queen of every span—her muslin, leaves, a sonic green,
       around her twigs, Ghent lace,
          we nest in fullness,
       servants before her sweeping branches.

All the other trees bend their heads—before her girth, time dances,
April pirouettes to the pulse—
          Lord Shiva's foot suspended, loosed on the air
Mistress Mahalakshmi,
       anima, animus, Mistress Tree
          on time's high waters, the hours lose their sleepy face,
       she drips and spills and points to evening
          her stems unfold
to dusk
       blossoms vibrate to far-off galaxies,
          Mother-Father tree
             she is sailing to the moon—

First page of the cover story in *Rolling Stone* magazine, July 1977.

PARTY PIECE

MY FIRST CEILIDH WAS IN IRELAND DURING THE ANNUAL BEEKEEPING WEEK hosted by the Federation of Irish Beekeeping Associations. Beekeepers from within and outside of Ireland have gathered each summer for over seventy years to take courses, hear lectures, attend workshops, compete in the National Honey Show and generally immerse themselves in everything bee. I was their keynote guest in 2003, and the three hundred or so beekeepers attending were most hospitable. One night I was invited to a kitchen party, the ceilidh of legend, a signature Irish evening where pints of Guinness flow and the entertainment is homegrown.

Many of those attending were lifelong friends, having participated in countless ceilidhs together, and each was expected to perform their signature party piece. Foreseeing what was coming only enhanced the group's enthusiasm as they singled out each performer to come up, the crowd yelling raucously with appreciation before, during and after each familiar contribution.

One exceedingly elderly gentleman, Seamus, was sitting in the back, shrunk into his seat. People kept calling him up; most had heard his party piece many times before, and he was obviously a crowd favourite. He ignored their exhortations for most of the night, but finally, after almost everyone had performed and the crowd's urgings had reached fever pitch, Seamus stood up.

Seamus was beyond old, ancient really, barely able to drag himself forward, the trip of perhaps thirty feet taking him an eternity to traverse. He did eventually reach the front of the room and turned to face the crowd. The years dropped away, his hunched-over demeanor expanding to full height much like a bicycle pump inflates a flat tire. Then, in a shockingly voluminous tenor voice, he began singing "Some Enchanted Evening," his stock-in-trade ceilidh party piece. The formerly boisterous partygoers fell silent as the room overflowed with sound, the young Seamus emerging from inside his used-up body. We remained transfixed as he sang, finished, deflated back to ancient and slowly shuffled to reclaim his seat at the rear of the room.

We academics also have signature pieces we bring out when invited to the professorial version of a ceilidh, delivering a lecture at a conference or university. As a graduate student during the late 1970s, I knew I had to develop a talk to impress if invited to an interview for one of the few coveted faculty positions available to young academics.

I had achieved that other milestone of academia, publishing a key paper, "Intra-colony Demography and Reproductive Rate of the Africanized Honey Bee in South America," in a top-tier prestigious journal, *Behavioral Ecology and Sociobiology* (*BES*). Demography is the study of how births, deaths and reproduction contribute to population growth or decline. It's most commonly used to build life tables with which insurance companies set rates, government develops policy and industry predicts consumer trends. The same tools can be used to study animals, and for honeybees could provide insights into how colonies grow and eventually split to reproduce by swarming. My Ph.D. research had studied whether individual worker lifespans change as colonies grow, and if so whether that contributed to the ability of the African bees to swarm at high and unprecedented rates compared to European bees.

I hoped this breakthrough *BES* publication would trigger that all-important interview on the path to employment. It hadn't been going well up to that point. I'd applied for many jobs, and as a self-belittling joke had wallpapered my University of Kansas office wall with rejection letters. I had reached close to fifty rejections when one day I received another one from Yale University for a job I hadn't even applied for. But fortunately the *BES* piece led to two interviews, both in Canada. Humbled by my poor interview track record so far, I spent endless hours honing my party piece.

The traditional way to deliver a talk was a straight-up data dump, showing slide after slide of graphs and tables and numbers, but I feared that might not be enough to land that elusive university job. I sought to craft a Seamus, a presentation finely honed by practice and tempered by experience, replete with tempo and rhythm, a performance more than a lecture. It didn't hurt that a year's worth of research had yielded a treasure trove of data that could be condensed into a simple and compelling scientific story. We had learned that the tropical African bees' signature for success was their high swarming rate, two to three times that of their temperate zone European cousins.

Both subspecies had been introduced into North and South America, and expressed the traits originally evolved in their respective European and African habitats. The European survival strategy was to invest energy in constructing large colonies in well-insulated tree cavities and swarm only once a year, in order to amass sufficient honey to survive cold winters. The African bees evolved in tropical climates where cold winters were not a factor, and had evolved a different strategy. They constructed small colonies, often just hanging exposed from tree branches, and swarmed many times a year, which worked because there was no need to store copious amounts of honey for the winter.

. The currency that fuelled their frequent swarming habit turned out to be worker lifespan, which increased in colonies as they grew. The first workers to emerge from newly founded colonies had short lifespans of twelve days on average, working themselves to death at young ages in service of rapid colony growth. When honeycomb construction was completed and the first new workers emerged, average lifespans lengthened to eighteen, then twenty-one days as worker bees began performing work at a less hectic pace. These extended lifespans resulted in a surplus of young underemployed worker bees within about two months after colony establishment, allowing swarming with these excess youngsters who served as the core workforce to establish new colonies.

This was an elegant scientific story, supported by the requisite graphs to withstand the scrutiny of a critical academic audience. But colony demography had considerably more texture, ranging from its implications for the spread and success of African bees to an adventure story with khaki-clad tropical biologists at its centre. Mixed into the research were stories about tragic fatalities from incidents of massive stinging as well as personal reflections from my prolonged South American immersion into the life of another species.

I added storytelling to travel beyond the data towards the broader picture that surrounds scientific tales but often is excluded from academic talks. I included photos showing scenes of our jungle/savannah research sites and our killer bee team capturing swarms, alluded matter-of-factly to our sensationalized bravery in the face of stinging incidents of epic proportions and dropped hints about how our work had crossed the "ivory tower" boundary to public media, including a cover story in *Rolling Stone* magazine.

As well, the talk extracted policy implications gleanable from the data. I talked about why the African bees' rapid colony growth and swarming doomed any attempt to stop their northward movement into the most southern United States, and how the same characteristics would prohibit the bees from surviving further north. I dipped into the biology of invasive species, marvelling at how perfectly pre-adapted the African bees were to South American habitats, so that their introduction and rate of spread put them at the pinnacle of success stories for any introduced animal or plant.

My job interview talk must have been a reasonably perky party piece because it landed me two offers, including the position at Simon Fraser University where I've been since 1980. At the time I thought my lecture was pushing the boundaries of science culture, but after seeing Seamus's performance I realized I could have dived further below science's shallow waters to more profound depths.

We scientists too often stop at the analysis, halted by some unspoken professional barrier that excludes the broader perspectives residing beneath the numbers. Superlative science communication begins with clear, objective explanation, but is at its richest when reflecting on the most personal and profoundly incomprehensible questions: who are we, why are we here, what do we believe, where do our responsibilities lie?

Seamus's song took the ceilidh from the mundane to the imaginative, opening a window into the unexpected passion prowling beneath the outer wall of his age-depleted body. Similarly, intra-colony demography was but a surface expression of what lay beneath. My data were a numerical representation of the altruistic sacrifices social organisms make for their communities. African bee lifespans may be simple numbers, but they articulate the core dilemma of sociality, balancing individual success with that of their colony.

Honeybee behaviours most often favour colony over individual; my demographic research revealed worker bees render the ultimate sacrifice by shortening their own lives to work harder for queen and colony. With hindsight, I now see that my data revealed a more meaningful picture than I had imagined of how selfless behaviour creates communal prosperity through the crucible of individual sacrifice. Honeybees have persisted for forty million years based on that simple trade-off between individual accomplishment and the greater good, a celebration of the enduring splendour of survival.

Consequences, this shift
Swarms populated, young workers
Colony and growth, those rates
Thus partly and determined
What the word endurance means.

HOLLOW WAX

that nest architecture, brood, cells, the years
vertical, conical, newly emerged
colony where workers reared, hollow wax

colony where workers reared, hollow wax
from May to July, nectar in the field
that nest architecture, brood, cells, the years

that nest architecture, brood, cells, the years
if fewer than, no comb at all, those swarms
colony where workers reared, hollow wax

colony where workers reared, hollow wax
small cages, double-layered nylon bags
that nest architecture, brood, cells, the years

that nest architecture, brood, cells, the years
between the year [   ] and [   ], data pooled
colony, where workers reared, hollow wax

in the lower corners, October days
old queen in her nest that one season, gone—
that nest architecture, brood, cells, the years
colony, where workers reared, hollow wax

HEXED

of surface and perimeter
both proximate and ultimate
first the circle, then—
possible, pressure or
soft, that wax moulded
three times and angled

convergence, a triple junction
between and adjacent
or shape not heat—
all their mysteries.
Isodiametric
cylindrical

tight-packed
surrounded
same-sized
those margins
stubbed, in the groove
and asking how—

and searching,
we saw them
add small, the wax
scale to scale
those builders
removed

from the base, a collective
hundreds, arrayed, aligned
linear—if this, then—
tip to tip, even with error
regular, wall to floor
left, right, yes or—

we removed them with smoke
the frame placed, central
we photographed, observing
that apiary, where, and—
those hours spent, a slight breeze
that summer—

Swarm coming in bedroom window in French Guiana, 1976, photo by Mark Winston.

SWARMING

I WAS LYING IN THE HAMMOCK I USED AS A DUAL-PURPOSE BED AND CHAIR in my sparsely furnished French Guiana bedroom when a swarm flew in the window and colonized an empty hive box we had stored there. That's all it took. I immediately developed an obsessive interest in everything to do with swarming, driving much of my research in South America and then in Canada for the next couple of decades.

Swarming is the key to honeybee life history, with all aspects of colony growth oriented toward producing offspring. Colonies usually swarm in the spring in temperate climates, but throughout most of the year in the tropics. A bit over half of the worker bees and the old queen leave the nest and settle under a tree limb or other overhang. Then, during the next few days, scout bees look for a new nest site. Once they find a suitable location the cluster takes to the air and flies to their new home. Back in the mother colony, new queens emerge and mate, so that the original colony continues as well.

The issuing of a swarm is one of nature's most spectacular events. All is quiet up to a few minutes before swarming, with festoons of bees hanging from the bottoms of comb and out the colony entrance. Suddenly waves of bees run back and forth in a coordinated flow, stimulated by a vibration dance conducted by some of the workers. The queen is bitten and chased out of the hive, joining a majority of worker bees in a cluster that soon quiets to conduct the necessary business of searching for a new nest site.

Considerable research has been focused on the swarm itself, particularly in how the clustering bees send out scouts, find a new site and move cross-country to their new home. It is an exquisitely complex event requiring a high level of coordination and communication, well worth the attention it's received. But the months prior to swarming are equally elegant if less spectacular, symphonic in having a series of movements that gradually build into the crescendo of swarming, followed by a slow denouement. These events in the hive, lasting many months, have their own beautiful rhythm and synchrony, exquisitely timed to maximize the survival of both the swarm and the mother colony.

Our methodology in studying the colony factors relevant to swarming was to take copious measurements before, during and after swarms issued, including any factors that might affect decisions to rear queens and subsequently swarm. We weighed colonies and the swarms we caught and assessed key life-history components every few days, including measuring the area of brood (eggs, larvae and pupae), honey, pollen and total comb the colonies had constructed. Since our interest was in life history, we didn't manage the colonies at all, but let them swarm, or not, on their own.

Tedious, laborious measurements were our bread and butter, but catching the swarms themselves was the fun part. Capturing swarms was essential to determine how many swarms each colony produced, the numbers of bees that issued or stayed behind in each swarm, and the workers' ages. We also wanted to follow the hived swarms and the home colony to determine their growth and success when swarming was completed. Our mantra was "no swarm shall escape us," and to accomplish that objective we learned to tolerate long periods of waiting punctuated by acrobatic positioning to catch swarms when they issued and settled. It was often a two-person job, one of us hanging precariously from a tree limb and shaking the branch, while the other was underneath with a mesh bag to catch the shaken swarm. We could then weigh the bag with swarm, and dump the bees into an empty box as their new domicile.

The first thing we learned is that seasonal timing is everything. Preparations to swarm begin with rearing broods in the dead of winter in temperate climates, so that colonies can grow to large enough populations to swarm by mid-spring. Early swarming is important to provide sufficient time for the swarm to build a nest with sufficient comb to store the forty to sixty pounds of honey they need to survive the next winter, and also for the mother colony to recover from losing most of its adult bees.

We were also able to resolve a key issue in swarming, what stimulates colonies to rear queens, which they must do prior to the old queen leaving with the first swarm. Our hypothesis, confirmed by two experiments, was that congestion builds as worker populations grow, inhibiting the transmission of the queen's pheromone that in less-crowded conditions inhibits the worker bees from rearing queens.

In the first experiment, we tracked radioactively labelled pheromone moving through congested and uncongested colonies. We discovered that only about 50 percent of worker bees encountered the queen's pheromone in congested colonies, compared to over 90 percent in uncongested colonies. The second experiment involved adding excess amounts of synthetic queen pheromone to colonies on glass slides spread throughout the nest, which resulted in almost all worker bees encountering queen pheromone even when colonies were highly congested. With that excess pheromone, colonies delayed queen rearing and swarming by over a month, again indicating the pivotal role the queen's message has in swarm preparation.

Worker age is also important. We built life table models of worker age distributions by marking thousands of young bees with coloured and numbered labels at weekly intervals, and then conducting a census of marked workers every seven days by examining all the frames in each colony early in the morning before foraging bees left the hive. With these data, plus regular assessments of colony populations, we could determine how many workers of what ages were present in colonies before and after queen rearing and swarming. When queen rearing begins, about half of the workers are less than eight days old, functionally important in providing a surplus of young nurse bees to rear queens and workers. It's not clear whether there's a behavioural signal by which workers assess their age distribution; perhaps pheromone drop is enough, as congestion is correlated with that burst in emergence of younger bees. Or perhaps swarming is an outlet for the pent-up energy of too many adolescent bees with too little to do and time on their hands.

Because we had so many worker bees marked in each colony, we could determine the ages of who left with the swarm and who stayed behind in the mother colony. Once we hived the swarm, we painstakingly went through the newly hived colony and the parental colony to find and record the numbers of all the marked bees. On average, 70 percent of workers leaving with the swarm were under the age of ten days old. This skewed probability towards younger bees issuing with the swarm is critically important for swarm survival, as the new swarm needs young bees to build comb and rear their first brood. Too many older foraging bees with short lifespans would leave the new colony critically short of worker bees after a week or two, and unable to begin growing quickly enough to survive the coming winter.

But what of the home colony, now deprived of young bees? Here, too, colonies have an elegant solution, since a considerable amount of eggs, larvae and pupae are left behind to repopulate the original colony. At the point of swarming, 90–95 percent of cells in the brood area are filled, so that colony populations are quickly restored even before a new queen begins laying eggs.

One of the startling results from our research was that this wasn't the end of the swarming story. Beekeepers had occasionally reported subsequent swarms called "casts" or "afterswarms," smaller swarms that issued with the first virgin to emerge from a queen cell. But their frequency was thought to be rare. Not so; on average one to two afterswarms issue from colonies, and up to four, with higher frequency in warmer regions and from more populous colonies. We had to spend considerably more time in apiaries than we had anticipated catching these afterswarms, but it was well worth it for the cascade of data they produced.

The last component of our swarming cycle research was to follow the survival of both the swarms and the colonies from which they came. The survival rate for prime swarms can be as low as zero in the wet coastal climate of British Columbia, and as high as almost 80 percent for tropical African bees in South America. The average for temperate climates hovers around 25 percent survival through the first year. Survival rates are considerably higher for established colonies after that first year, close to 90 percent in all the habitats we and others studied. We calculated the birth (swarms) and death rates of colonies, and determined that wild honeybee colonies in temperate habitats have fairly stable populations, with little if any overall growth in the number of wild colonies. In the South American tropics, however, the colonizing African bees showed an astounding annual population growth of 6900 percent.

That is, starting with one colony, there would be seventy after a year, because that colony and then its offspring would each swarm three to four times a year, producing a prime swarm and two or three afterswarms each time they swarm, with about 80 percent survival of each new colony. With population growth that high, it's not surprising that these bees quickly colonized South and Central America, and the southern United States, soon establishing large permanent feral populations.

Our many years of swarming research crystallized my perception of honeybees as a decentralized rather than a hierarchical system, much like an orchestra but without a conductor. A swarm is an ensemble piece that weaves individual contributions into a symphony much larger than its parts, with clearly defined movements.

To my surprise I realized the "Swarm Symphony" has already been written, although the composer didn't have bees in mind, and his inspiration was frequent trips to country villages rather than to apiaries. It was Ludwig von Beethoven's "Symphony No. 6," better known as the "Pastoral" symphony, the inspiration and music used in the classic animated Disney film *Fantasia*. The five movements of the "Pastoral" align well with how swarming develops from winter through spring. The first movement, titled "Awakening," presents the themes and melodies of the piece, and refers to arriving in the pastoral countryside. In my imagined "Swarm Symphony" the colony awakens by initiating brood rearing during the heart of winter, anticipating the onset of spring.

Beethoven's second movement is titled "Scene by the Brook," its motif of flowing water reminiscent of the placid but quickening spring during which colonies grow. His third movement, "Merry Gathering of Country Folk," is a fast tempo section depicting peasants dancing. The hive's third movement begins with queen rearing, as colonies become congested and the pre-swarming hive tempo speeds up to its inevitable denouement. The "Pastoral" fourth movement is "Thunder, Storm." Here the hive is disrupted as thousands of bees take to the air with a deafening buzz before settling into a cluster and seeking a new nest. Finally, there is the fifth movement "Cheerful and Thankful Feelings After the Storm," when colonies are re-established and harmony returns.

What's most remarkable about the orchestration of swarming is that there is no conductor, but rather thousands of bees making local choices about what tasks to perform that lead to the communal decision to swarm. Still, the symphony played by our colony orchestra is well coordinated without a conductor; queen pheromone provides the underlying melody. Her odour contributes to a complex piece of music indeed, strong at the beginning of the season, slowly diminishing as congestion interferes with its notes, absent from the concerto when the swarm finally issues and the old queen departs, and then reestablished strongly at the end of the opus when the new queen mates and begins her reign.

Like any good orchestra playing a classic symphony, the collaborative interaction of many bees ascends to a contribution considerably greater than its component parts. Each bee has a role, minuscule on her own but together creating the stunning melodies and underlying rhythms that have driven honeybee survival for tens of millions of years.

The word "symphony" is Greek in origin, meaning "agreement or concord of sound," as well as "harmonious." The ancient Greeks used it as a term for consonance as opposed to dissonance, and it's that amenable societal resonance, illustrated by swarming, that most fascinates us about honeybees.

FIELD NOTES OF THE PARTICULAR

(a)

growth described
colonies and the influence
rate of workers, their production
reproductive cycles, post-emergence
the number of afterswarms
survivorship for both brood and—
also shifts during
thus partly determine(d)

(b)

in a social insect such as the honeybee
and thus intra-colony, the growth rate
however, the role of these factors

in 1956, twenty-six queens of the African
Apis mellifera scutellata, formerly
had been brought to Brazil for—

their escape, their feral colonies
high colony densities, South America
by such "r-selected" traits

(c)

during the swarming season
near Kourou, French Guiana
August 1976–February 1977

fewer than fifteen colonies
of European bees in all of
when the Africanized arrived

extremely similar to—
and from South Africa
our personal communication

(d)

marked cohorts of one hundred newly emerged
were placed into study colonies
at ten-day intervals, beginning on the
after a colony established
when the first new young and emerged

cohorts were obtained
combs removed from other hives
in the apiaries, allowing workers
to emerge, sealed pupal cells
within one or two hours

(e)

consequences, this shift
swarms populated, young workers
colony and growth, those rates
thus partly and determined

Mark Winston in tropical biology field course, island of Bimini, 1971,
photographer unknown.

Swarm Team, 1988, photographer unknown.

SWARM TEAM

I LEARNED MY EARLIEST LESSON ABOUT SUPERVISING STUDENTS FROM PHIL, who joined my lab to study swarming just after I arrived as a new faculty member at Simon Fraser University (SFU) in 1980. Phil seemed like a talented student, whose strong grades and rapid-fire mind were good qualities in a student. It didn't hurt that he was also was an expert impersonator, with an imitation of Asian Elvis at the top of his repertoire. One year towards the end of his time in my lab he was inspired by a challenge from the other students to impersonate a deer filling out a deposit slip in a bank. It's impossible to describe, except to say that for a moment he did become a deer filling out a deposit slip—perhaps the funniest thing I've ever seen.

Given his speedy firing-on-all-cylinders brain, I thought Phil would be quick to acquire the skills needed to study swarming. I was disappointed when I went out with him day after day and he seemed dull, slow to benefit from my considerable experience, and generally unenthusiastic about the tedium of measuring and waiting. I grumbled to my wife each night about Phil, until finally she suggested I stay back in my university office and let Phil go out on his own. The next day, to his surprise and mine, I sent him off without the benefit of my watching over his shoulder. His return to the lab late that afternoon was memorable; Phil ran into the room carrying a buzzing swarm in a mesh bag, talking a mile a minute about how he caught it, fired up with as much enthusiasm as he revealed doing his deer-in-the-bank imitation.

I let Phil go out on his own after that, with great success. Now he could see the benefits of the tedious measuring and waiting that occupied most of his research time, with a newfound patience made worthwhile by those punctuated moments of swarming excitement. It's a key pivot point when running a laboratory, or any organization for that matter, deciding how much to do yourself and how much to trust your people. That day with Phil was my first tentative step toward understanding what being a mentor is all about, taking my hands off so my students could put their own hands on.

Like most new faculty members, I hadn't acquired much experience in teaching or mentoring graduate students while I myself was a student. I had progressed through the usual post-Ph.D. academic pathway, first as a postdoctoral fellow for a year in which I essentially continued my doctoral research, and then on to a one-year temporary job at Idaho State University in Pocatello, replacing a faculty member who was on sabbatical leave that year.

My naiveté when I arrived as an assistant professor at SFU was palpable, particularly about the business side of running a lab. For example, university science departments typically offer start-up funds for new faculty to purchase equipment and supplies to get their laboratory up and running. When the chair of my new home at the Department of Biological Sciences asked me what I needed to get going, all I could think to ask for was an electric typewriter, and he promptly had a used one wheeled into my new office. It hadn't occurred to me that I would need bees, beekeeping equipment, glassware, microscopes and the other accoutrements necessary to populate an entomology laboratory.

I smartened up eventually, and fortunately my department chair was a merciful soul who found some funds for me to purchase about twenty colonies of bees, the hives to put them in, bee suits, veils and the equipment needed to extract the honey that would soon fill my colonies. But I'd forgotten another important issue: university laboratories are not exactly set up for beekeeping, which requires at least a pickup truck, a honey house in which to build and store equipment and a place to extract and bottle the honey. And I needed an isolated bee yard close to the university where we could keep our bees without them annoying anyone passing by.

I soon became adept at working around the margins of university facilities, finding those rundown and isolated outposts that everyone had forgotten but would serve my beekeeping needs nicely. First, we moved into a trailer slated for demolition to make way for a new wing of the chemistry department, but since universities move slowly we were able to stay there for almost a decade undisturbed. Eventually the demolition began, so I found an abandoned building at the edge of the university that had previously been a broadcast facility for a local television station. SFU is up on a mountain, and altitude greatly improved the distance broadcast signals could travel in the bygone days of analog. We had the building renovated to meet our beekeeping and research needs, and the Bee House became research central for the next twenty years.

So now I had beehives, a laboratory and a honey house, but I still needed the most important component of all: students. Here I had the good fortune that my core teaching assignment was BISC 317, a third-year introductory entomology course. I gleaned my first five graduate students from the initial fall 1980 offering, jump-starting my lab and getting our research off to a flying start.

· We called ourselves the Swarm Team, and mid-summer every year took an official photo followed by lunch at a nearby all-you-can-eat sushi restaurant, funded by the revenue from the previous year's honey harvest. We had many traditions, all involving food: a highly competitive annual cheesecake contest, a summer barbecue at colleague Keith Slessor's country home and winter equipment building parties in the Bee House fueled by pizza.

Transitioning from being a student responsible only for myself to running a lab with up to twenty-five students and staff was a challenge. Fortunately, I had the bees to guide me. The decades I spent immersed in swarms left me with deep respect for the complexity and adaptive capacities of honeybees, but also had a defining impact on how I managed my growing laboratory. I developed a decentralized rather than a hierarchical management style that emphasized collaboration and cooperation, similar to honeybee swarming. A research laboratory is also orchestral, like swarming, an ensemble that weaves individual contributions into a unit much greater than its parts. My job as conductor was not to play the instruments, but simply to set the tempo, leaving room for the students' own interpretations and styles.

We had many students with distinct projects, each requiring a labour force at different times of the year. Each student had to ponder the tasks that needed to be done, organize work parties at peak times and manage their own time to be available during other students' labour-heavy phases. Attention to how honeybees approach their complex and seasonally based swarming cycle provided a model for how myriad individuals can perform their own work that adds up into a communal-level success considerably greater than its parts.

A typical season would begin with the entire lab out in the field counting bees pollinating blueberries in the spring, then switch to measuring colonies prior to and during swarming. We'd return to blueberry fields in the summer to pick and weigh the berries visited by various bee species, followed by a fall/winter work party to identify the wild bees we had collected. Throughout the spring to fall we would do pheromone identification work in the laboratory and conduct experiments in colonies. Winter found all of us writing up our research and planning the next season's projects. Finally, imposed on the science was running a two hundred–colony apiary, with each season bringing its own particular beekeeping work.

I'd also learned the value of effective communication from the bees, a key underpinning for any successful society. Information transfer is key, and we had weekly lab meetings to review projects, allocate work and provide feedback for students stuck on knotty research issues.

Honeybees communicate primarily through pheromones and their dance language, but graduate students communicate through writing and speaking. Right from the start we emphasized revision, providing epic feedback on publication drafts and early versions of talks. For writing, the red pen was my tool, and numerous versions of papers went back and forth before submission, until the red ink was no longer needed. To prepare for presentations to other scientists, beekeepers or the public, students would present a practice version to the entire laboratory. It became a rite of passage to participate in these feedback sessions; while I never permitted unkind comments, it was in the students' best interests to hear rigorous but supportive critique. As a result, their talks became known throughout the various communities we served for their quality and impact.

Early on I'd also learned something important from beekeepers: the importance of public interaction. After all, our funding came primarily from taxpayers, and I wanted my students to recognize our responsibility to communicate our research to an audience wider than just our fellow scientists. I sent the students out to innumerable beekeeping meetings, school visits and garden clubs, in addition to the usual round of provincial/state, national and international scientific meetings that entomologists traditionally attend. Their public outreach vastly improved their scientific presentations, as addressing audiences of non-experts teaches speakers to avoid jargon, simplify messages and use compelling visual aids. Between us we delivered fifty to one hundred talks a year, an invaluable experience for young students working to find their voices in the world.

I came to see the Swarm Team as an extension of the hive, and of the wild bees we also studied. At one level our nickname was cute, but underneath the name were reflective lessons in human interaction. Much as honeybees collaborate to create an entity larger than its parts, my students benefited greatly from fitting their solitary goals into the communal framework of the Swarm Team. Just as honeybee societies depend on effective communication, the students learned how being strong writers and speakers could be the wings through which their own individual voices could develop and soar. But they also learned the deep satisfaction that comes from interacting effectively with the public, a distinctive fulfillment arising from contributing to something outside their own narrow fields of study.

Wild bees are characterized by their wide diversity, and here too my students gleaned important lessons by listening to the bees. Pollination is most effective when many different bee species visit flowers, and research similarly benefits from the collective wisdom of diverse perspectives. It was surprising how often a student studying blueberry pollination would get an idea from our swarm research, or a pheromone project would influence a study about honeybee diseases and pests.

There came a time when each student finished their work, wrote up their publications, defended their degrees and graduated. Their departures were usually punctuated with appreciation for their faculty supervisors and fellow students, and any beekeepers or growers who had helped them along the way. But they would become notably emotional when expressing gratitude to the bees, strikingly appreciative for having established a lasting connection to some of the other species with which we inhabit our planet. They took that appreciation onward in their lives, forever changed by their time with the bees as much as with each other.

In that way the laboratory was a hearing aid, amplifying the subtle messages to be learned when we listen, truly listen, to the bees.

CAPTURED

i.

double-layered

that nylon

they bagged her

queen, after swarming

placed cage upon cage

each, weighed—

hived, those standard ten frames

and said—*Langstroth*

wax strips, along the top

to guide the comb—

that nylon

double-layered

ii.

clear plastic grids
square over square

broods, sided, sealed
cells in centimetres

five by five
for all colonies, the years—

iii.

autumn, winter—
    square over square
        from the time of the queen's death—

iv.

no statistical   differences
could be found   between
for any of   the parameters measured

v.

double-layered
to guide the comb
clear plastic grids
for all colonies, the years
from the time of—
Come, they said—

THE BEEKEEPER'S LAMENT

Said the Beekeeper

"O bring me my palanquin
All my companions have scattered"

ALL MY COMPANIONS HAVE SCATTERED. WHAT AN APT DESCRIPTOR OF A beekeeper entering an apiary to find the bees gone, the colonies dead. It's not unusual to visit an apiary of, say, twenty colonies and find one or two in demise. Colonies pass on for many reasons: they run out of honey, the queen dies, a bear knocks over the hive in pursuit of the colony's larvae, hornets attack in the fall, a disease sweeps through. Sad, yes, but the remaining colonies provide an optimistic balance to the day, and beekeepers learn to accept and learn from the occasional colony loss.

But this is different, what's been happening for the last decade. A bee-keeper walks into an apiary and finds almost every colony dead, the bees disappeared, with only a wistful few workers left bereft in the hive, confused by the disappearance of what only weeks before had been their thriving community. And it's often much worse. Commercial beekeepers may manage one thousand colonies, or ten thousand, sometimes keeping many hundreds or thousands of hives together in one apiary during the winter before dispersing them for spring pollination contracts. Imagine walking into apiary after apiary to find half your colonies dead. For some, the experience has been numerically even more catastrophic, with losses of 80 or 90 percent of previously healthy hives.

We know the cause: a perfect storm of pesticide impact, lack of nectar and pollen producing plants in the field and increased abundance and virulence of disease and pests. The precise pesticide, nutritional deficit and disease/pest may differ from apiary to apiary, region to region, but the overall picture is consistent: synergy between these factors has overwhelmed the considerable resilience of honeybee colonies, and colony fatality is rampant. Chaos and catastrophe abound, and despair among beekeepers proliferates along with the widespread loss of their colonies.

Some of their anguish is commercial, as they see their livelihood disappear along with their bees. But income is not the only foundation of beekeeper despair; our attachment to bees is profound, and massive loss overwhelms our emotional capacity to cope with loss.

The beekeeper's lament is not so much a dirge as it is the lack of sound, the diminution of that characteristic buzzing noise that permeates the air of a healthy apiary. There's a moment of heartbreak entering a too-quiet apiary, the rising bile of despair, overwhelmed with the extent of cataclysmic tragedy.

We feel, deeply, the demise of our bees, and mourn them as we would any profound loss. But successful beekeepers are also practical by nature, and before too long we get up and begin gathering the dead hives, loading them onto our trucks and returning to the honey house where we'll clean them up and prepare the hives to start new colonies. We, like our bees, are resilient, and while the loss is palpable, the future beckons. Soon the apiary is restocked with young colonies, but entering an apiary is never as innocent as before. Now we understand that at any visit we may find that our companions have scattered, and the prosperous buzz of a healthy apiary turned yet again to a song of lament.

WOULD NOT CATCH

morning and those foragers
      coming and going

coming and going
      and then, and then

landed, substrate, edge
      and ran, wings buzzed
          and ran,
and ran
their *gasters,* held low—waggling
      waggling
and then all, faster
         faster
large arcs-   larger larger—passing only to hover,
downwind
      where the many moved
         so diffuse—through,
           between,
              across, a-
              part—

we walked that path, stood,
    —unaware—

HONEY-COMBED & PRISM

January blooms
Mahonia, high evergreen
foliage spiked,
who would foreshadow summer
in the shade
April whan those showeres sweete
thrift—grassy clumps—
clustered pink, bright
brighter than those pale
cranesbill, woodland rows
open meadows, where
low and doubled, columbine
smothered in—or, silvery
bugloss, edge of the path
footsteps crushing orange-spice-thyme
tiny, between paving stones
rocky outcrops, May loving sedum
stacked against rosettes, fringe cups
till June's foxglove, nestled-fanned-spread,
those endless afternoons
July—catmint, *Nepeta,* grey leaves
a-buzz, and all a-yellow
tick seed mounds
late summer farewells
those we'd never see
come while a-way
Michaelmas daisies
who bowed their heads
goldenrod, sea holly,

blue petals, tall thistles
come August of the open meadows
purple cornflower, speedwell spires and—

EVERYTHING OLD IS NEW AGAIN

I'M PARTIAL AS A WRITER TO CERTAIN WORDS, PARTICULARLY THOSE infused by my own experiences and memories that go well beyond dictionary definitions. So it has been with "pastoral," defined as "pertaining to the country, rural, rustic, idyllic," and the "giving of spiritual guidance." I used to couple "beekeeping" with "pastoral," and my early experiences and those of beekeepers in my generation tended to the rural, idyllic and spiritual. The apiaries we visited in those days were often at the end of country dirt roads, located by scenic, slow-flowing riverbanks and shaded by large trees—the bee-loud glades of Yeats come alive.

And the honeybees, well, they almost kept themselves, requiring little in the way of maintenance and afflicted with few diseases and pests requiring our attention. Flowers were abundant in the fields and forests within flying distance of our colonies, and through our bees and the nectar and pollen they collected, we learned the natural ebb and flow of the seasons. There was an art to beekeeping that could be mastered, deep satisfaction in applying skills and experience to solve any problems that arose.

Fast-forward to today, and "pastoral" is a less compatible fit with "honeybee." Beekeeping is no longer idyllic, the art of it no longer sufficient to overcome the myriad issues confronting colonies. It's been a slow erosion, caused by a toxic mix of environmental change and the drift of beekeeping towards a more industrial complexion. Agricultural pesticide use has increased and floral abundance has diminished due to habitat changes and extensive single-crop acreages. These environmental changes have forced beekeepers to take on prodigious pollination contracts to make ends meet, moving colonies cross-country multiple times each year. Their colonies end up parked for a few weeks at a time in what to a bee appears as an agricultural desert rather than the mixed floral habitats they experienced in the countryside surrounding those bee-loud glades.

Diseases and pests afflicting honeybees have also exploded, particularly viral outbreaks transmitted and activated by the introduced varroa mite pest.

Formerly pesticide-averse beekeepers have found themselves dosing and then overdosing their hives with miticides, fungicides and antibiotics. Not surprisingly, honeybee diseases and pests have become resistant to many of the synthetic chemicals that have come to define beekeeping practices today.

The advent of this industrial beekeeping, characterized by beekeepers who run tens of thousands of colonies from the beds of flatbed trucks, did not happen suddenly. It grew slowly over many decades along with diminishing natural habitats and increasing corporate-sized agriculture, exacerbated by extensive movement of honeybee colonies that transported invasive diseases and pests across countries and between continents.

No beekeeper, no matter how competent or talented, has been able to keep their colonies even remotely as healthy as they were decades ago. Back then perhaps 5 to 10 percent of honeybee colonies died each year, compared to today's average 35 to 45 percent annual colony fatality rate.

But an odd thing has been happening recently. I travel extensively to beekeeping meetings, and I've noticed a pattern emerging that is on the verge of transitioning into a movement. Beekeeping is being reinvented based on the old days, returning to the pastoral practices that were so healthy for bees and provided such satisfaction for beekeepers. By "old days," I mean both *really* old days, about forty million years ago, as well as slightly old days from the last few thousand years of human civilization. The really-old-days movement now has a name, Darwinian Beekeeping, referring to beekeepers who are looking to the biology of wild honeybee colonies to redesign colony management, disease control and apiary geography. The essence of this bee-friendly beekeeping is to let the bees live as naturally as possible, making use of the adaptations colonies have acquired over the last forty-million years, since the first honeybees evolved. Darwinian beekeepers are willing to accept lower yields per colony and forego moving honeybees for pollination in favour of improved colony health and survival as well as enhanced enjoyment for the beekeeper.

Wild honeybee colonies have numerous adaptations that have allowed them to survive in diverse habitats and could be adapted into managed hives. For example, industrial beekeeping today often crams hundreds of colonies into a single apiary site, with each colony stacked many boxes high and each box with thin uninsulated walls. In contrast, wild hives are highly dispersed, reducing the potential for disease/pest transmission and increasing the diversity and abundance of flowers available per colony. Their nests are most often in thick-walled hollow logs and tree cavities, insulated from both heat and cold, and small enough that colonies don't have to expend too much energy to thermoregulate. Darwinian beekeepers are modelling their management after these traits of feral colonies, with fewer hives per apiary, each hive smaller that the industrial sizes and hive walls that are better insulated than current versions.

Darwinian management practices also draw from the feral. Apiaries are stationary, with colonies rarely if ever moved for pollination or other purposes. Darwinian beekeepers also allow colonies to rear their own new queens and mate with local drones rather than having beekeepers introduce a purchased queen from another region. In that way, natural selection is utilized to select for colonies well adapted to local conditions.

Another Darwinian practice is treatment-free beekeeping, eliminating the ubiquitous pesticide treatments that have become pervasive in industrial beekeeping. Darwinians recognize that the heavy use of chemicals has prevented the evolution of natural resistance, and by foregoing treatments or using only natural substances that the bees themselves might encounter in the field, they are allowing those millions of years of honeybee evolution to provide solutions for disease and pest problems.

The bottom line for Darwinian beekeeping is simple: each colony produces less honey but is healthier, with improved survival. And, beekeepers who practice the Darwinian approach find deeper enjoyment in their craft by connecting to the idea of honeybees as feral organisms with a phenomenally long and rich evolutionary history.

Beekeeping is also being reimagined from ancient practices not quite as old as evolutionary time but drawing from similar ideas. The classical Roman poet Virgil preceded Darwin's idea of evolution by natural selection by a few thousand years, yet came to realizations consistent with those being promoted by Darwinian beekeepers.

Virgil's epic poem "Georgics" from 29 BCE contributed considerable wisdom relevant to our currently evolving ideas about more natural rather than industrial honeybee management. Virgil was well aware that selecting an apiary site protected from the weather, and constructing hives in which bees could easily control their internal colony temperature, were critical elements in managing honeybee colonies. He also appreciated the value of the pastoral, both for the bees' benefit as well as the enjoyment of the beekeepers:

> First look for a site and position for your apiary,
> where no wind can enter (since the winds prevent them

carrying home their food)…
Let the hives themselves have narrow entrances,
whether they're seamed from hollow bark,
or woven from pliant osiers: since winter congeals
the honey with cold, and heat loosens it with melting.
Either problem's equally to be feared with bees…
But let there be clear springs nearby, and pools green with moss,
and a little stream sliding through the grass,
and let a palm tree or a large wild-olive shade the entrance…

Virgil also was well attuned to habitat, understanding the need for diverse flowers near the apiary to provide adequate nutrition:

the twice-flowering rose-beds of Paestum,
how the endive delights in the streams it drinks,
and the green banks in parsley, and how the gourd, twisting
over the ground, swells its belly: nor would I be silent about
the late-flowering narcissi, or the curling stem of acanthus,
the pale ivy, and the myrtle that loves the shore.

His advice for beekeepers to use natural substances to treat against diseases and pests also resonates with beekeepers today who seek a less invasive relationship with their bees. Virgil recognized the signs of disease, understood that the plant resins wild bees collect to coat the nest with have medicinal properties (referred to in the lines below as "glue"), and promoted natural treatments when needed:

Since life has brought the same misfortunes to bees as ourselves,
if their bodies are weakened with wretched disease,
you can recognize it straight away by clear signs:
as they sicken their colour immediately changes: a rough
leanness mars their appearance: then they carry outdoors
the bodies of those without life, and lead the sad funeral procession…

it's not for nothing that they emulate each other in lining
the thin cells of their hives with wax, and filling the crevices
with glue made from the flowers, and keep a store of it
for this use, stickier than bird lime or pitch from Phrygian Ida…

I'd urge you to burn fragrant resin, right away,
and give them honey through reed pipes, freely calling them
and exhorting the weary insects to eat their familiar food.
It's good too to blend a taste of pounded oak-apples
with dry rose petals, or rich new wine boiled down
over a strong flame, or dried grapes from Psithian vines,
with Attic thyme and strong-smelling centaury.

Whatever its source, whether evolutionary biology or poetry, there is great wisdom available from the old days about how to keep bees. And it's progressing from a trend into a full-blown movement. Scientific research comparing Darwinian and industrial beekeeping is starting to appear in peer-reviewed journals, and anecdotal articles about new approaches abound in beekeeping magazines and newsletters. Organizations are forming, international conferences being held. Social media is replete with tweets, Instagrams and Facebook pages focused on bee-friendly approaches to management.

The pastoral culture of beekeeping is returning, with potential for impact far beyond bees into improving many aspects of our environmental stewardship. Past attitudes that emphasized the spiritual and personal benefits of beekeeping are being rediscovered, growing towards a crescendo proclaiming that healthy bees are the best way to ensure productivity.

The last few decades of beekeeping meetings have been infused with discussion about problems, but more positive conversations now pervade the podium and hallway conversations. Beekeepers are waxing poetic about how bees connect them spiritually to nature and the seasons. They celebrate the spirit of the hive with its depth of communal cooperation and important lessons about the value of collaboration. Many mention how the quiet, peace and calm of a well-tended apiary are counterbalances to an increasingly hectic and chaotic world.

The language of science is converging with the tongue of poetry, combining the skills generated by Darwinian beekeeping with the idyllic spirituality inspired by poets. The last few decades in the beekeeping world have been dominated by beekeepers pushing to get the most productivity out of their colonies at the expense of hive health. As a result, colonies have suffered and profitability has declined.

Everything old is new again with this powerful alliance between the Darwinian and the pastoral reminding us to look to the past for wisdom about how to manage in the future. The next generation promises to be one of greater balance, with the economic health of beekeeping more assured by a return to more pastoral paradigms. It's a simple lesson, one that applies to all aspects of how we manage the world around us, and one in which bees are serving as the bellwether organism. We beekeepers are recognizing that our future, and that of our bees, will be most assured by putting bee health first.

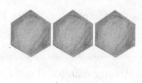

BEE-RAGA TO BHRAMARI DEVI

that mystical body covered yellow-black: bees-bees-bees-bees——

that magical swarm, orbed, pocket of, outlier, outlandish

that swirling——clouds skittish, wisps of batten——

that waxed-waning——Ishtar-Luna-Diana-Lakshmi and rose-gold

that honeypot overturned, bowstring and quiver, oak, maple, neem,

Banyan tree and under sits a woman with her blue sitar, red saree,

that golden disc, Cybele-Persephone, Deccan to Himalaya——

that white shadow in the sky, nail-bed thin, young or at horizon's edge

ecliptic-fat, orange——that harvest, pulsating fullness, patch and mend,

push, pull, millennia upon millennia, green-blue, midnight and black

pewter-silver-foxglove-metallic-white bone and bleached.

Tatiana, dust drifting down into ocean

that tune sung while wax is made, pollen scattered, gathered, brushed
that temple, a ship's captain, cat's eye, a low moss strewn tent
hook, awl, sextant and glove. That mendicant, itinerant, peddler and gypsy—
Rajasthan to Bombay, Calcutta to Pune—

that dawn's alba, evening sutra, cratered nests, thousands of cells
brood babies, foragers and workers, dandy males, bitten, ripped, killed

that wintering wolf, river inked, mountains massed,
small women made dervish at sundown. Hear our paean, riddles and gesture
broad circumference, six-sided and snug, whispered
secrets, hideaways, broom closets, too—heavy gourds. Gestating seed.
Cherry blossoms and withered floating leaves. A Rubik's Cube softened,
piñata smacked, everything round-misshapen-swollen

everything embraced—pale hands, brown skin, viola, cello, violin.
Concertina at dusk amid waggle and forward, backwards and up

Up, away and—

Bee Audacious conference, December 2016, photo by Sierra Salin.

BEE AUDACIOUS

I was at the most remarkable meeting in December 2016: "Bee Audacious: The Future of Bees, Beekeeping and Pollination." The meeting was a collaborative working conference that utilized dialogue to envision bold evidence-based ideas through which honeybees, other bees, beekeepers and pollination managers could prosper. The meeting demonstrated that not only is there much to be learned by listening to the bees, but there is also much to be gleaned from an assembly of beekeepers and wild bee enthusiasts.

These are not conventional times for bees, and the conventional wisdom about how to keep honeybees (*Apis mellifera*) and sustain non-*Apis* wild and managed pollinators no longer serves beekeepers, farmers or the critical societal imperative for environmental sustainability. The conference generated bold new ideas that encourage beekeepers to act as stewards of both managed and wild bees, promoters of healthy environments, managers of economically sustainable apiaries, supporters of diverse, effective pollination management systems, and paragons of collaboration and cooperation.

The meeting, held over two days at the Marconi Conference Center in Marshall, California, adopted the dialogue process we pioneered at Simon Fraser University's Centre for Dialogue. Dialogue is centred around concentrated conversation among equals, offering helpful ways to work together cooperatively, encouraging mutual understanding between diverse perspectives and leading to stable, resilient outcomes. Language matters, and how we talk together makes a difference. My work at the Centre for Dialogue was inspired by decades attending too many beekeeping and scientific meetings in which conflict became entrenched rather than resolved, or the meeting structure and agenda inhibited deeper personal discussion.

Meetings of beekeepers are rarely placid, gravitating to differences of opinion more often than finding common ground. Typically, one hothead stands up to discuss an issue with language that employs verbal barbs and dismissive rhetoric rather than more respectful, reflective wording. You know you're headed for trouble when that beekeeper gets up with the classic tactic to establish credibility: "My family has been keeping bees for four generations and…" Across the room a now-triggered beekeeper on a different side of the issue uses another well-worn tactic to establish his superior expertise, citing the high number of hives he runs in his commercial beekeeping business. In a flash, angry words have inflamed the room. Whatever issue is on the table polarizes, with speakers focusing on scoring points rather than listening to each other.

Scientific meetings tend to be more civil, but suffer from highly structured formats that inhibit dialogue. Presenters get up for tightly timed ten- or twenty-minute segments from early morning into the evening, each utilizing the same rigid talk layout. The "Introduction" tells the audience what research has been done in the past and how the current project will enhance knowledge, "Methods" outline how the work was done, "Results" provide complex and indigestible tables and graphs, and "Discussion" reminds us why the research was important. "Conclusions" usually promote the work that needs to be done next, establishing that this line of research is their territory and providing a rationale we'll soon see in the scientist's next grant application.

It's not a bad system to disseminate information, but beyond the occasional questions at the end of talks, there's little or no opportunity for discussion or more individual and intimate perspectives. We rarely see why scientists care, deeply, about pesticide impacts on bees, the diversity of wild pollinators or how social insects use pheromones to communicate. It's those fundamental personal motivations hidden deep beneath scientific jargon that are lacking, suppressed by training and the increasing reductionism of science that encourages contemporary scientists to separate who we are from what we do.

I began to think that there must be a better way to discuss contentious, emotionally charged issues, but my trajectory in dialogue accelerated while I was conducting research for my 2002 book *Travels in the Genetically Modified Zone*. I had become interested in GM crops because of their potential impact on bees, but my interest soon evolved toward understanding how controversial issues are debated in the arena of public opinion. My thinking about dialogue crystallized at an intense, three-day meeting in October 2000, conducted by the US Environmental Protection Agency in Crystal City, Virginia. The meeting was held to solicit public input on how GM crops would be regulated. I wrote a description of that experience in *Travels in the Genetically Modified Zone*:

The time I spent in that Crystal City hotel was among the most draining meeting experiences I have ever undergone. I left the meeting late Friday afternoon in a daze, and took the Metro into Washington, where I could decompress by wandering around on the spectacular urban parkland of Independence Mall. As I regained my composure, the source of my fatigue and disorientation gradually clarified. I had just spent three days being manipulated, with every hallway conversation and interview designed to shift my opinion, just as each submission to the panel members was intended to change their perception of the issues. The meeting room was a pressure cooker, with interest groups scheming to influence what went into the pot and how it was mixed. What was lacking was dialogue, an honest and straightforward exchange of views.

I moved to Simon Fraser University's downtown campus in 2002, and we began exploring how to best inhabit that gap in dialogue. In the ensuing years we've conducted hundreds of dialogues on many contentious issues, ranging from the very local (a fiery parking debate in the nearby town of Deep Cove) to the regional (priorities for transit) to the national (Canada's energy future) and even international (working with cities across the globe interested in committing to 100 percent renewable energy by 2050). But oddly, given my entomological interests, we had never organized a meeting about pollinator issues before Bee Audacious.

It finally occurred to me that, just as conventional wisdom about issues facing pollinators needed a serious rethink, meetings around those issues also required a reboot. The first step was to invite about a hundred participants from around the world who represented the many diverse perspectives through which pollinators are viewed. Most meetings are like attracting like; hobby beekeepers meet with other hobbyists, the commercial guys go to their own meetings, wild bee advocates don't sit down with honeybee keepers. We insured that the various segments were represented, with no group dominating.

The day before the meeting we brought in ten thought leaders, prominent individuals from both the scientific and beekeeping communities whom we trained to facilitate sessions at the meeting. The meeting was structured with none of the usual lecture-followed-by-questions-and-answers format, but rather we changed the audience into participants. The meeting rhythm emphasized facilitated breakouts with small groups of participants so that everyone's voice could be heard, followed by brief plenary reporting-out sessions with the entire conference. Extensive notes were taken to capture the full content of breakout discussions, which were incorporated into the final Bee Audacious report.

We began with a breakout about values, and over two days moved through issues concerning how honeybees were managed, the role of wild bees in agricultural systems, how to manage diseases and pests, innovative ways of earning income from pollinators and finally, approaches to organizing an effective lobbying effort. Throughout, we sought to emerge perspectives rather than jumping to argument and disagreement. Attitude proved to be as important as structure. We promoted curiosity as a guiding theme, and posed questions designed to yield collaborative inquiry rather than argument. Each participant's experience was valued as providing its own expertise; we were motivated by the core dialogue belief that collective wisdom is the best approach to cover the widest range of issues and yield the most resilient outcomes.

Storytelling was encouraged, and the personal perspectives we heard enriched the conversation immeasurably. We sought diverse solutions rather than a one-size-fits-all outcome, recognizing that there are multiple solutions required to meet the varied needs of pollinators as well as our multifaceted human imperatives for honey production and crop pollination.

The most audacious outcome from "Bee Audacious" was soon apparent—that those holding widely divergent points of view about bee and pollinator issues, perspectives that often appear in conflict, were able to collaborate and find broad areas of agreement. Beekeepers and wild bee enthusiasts may clash about managed pollination vs. the ecological services of wild bees, yet through dialogue reached agreement that all bees would benefit by improving pollinator habitats. Beekeepers militant about not treating their colonies with antibiotics and pesticides, and those who medicate against diseases and pests, have been on opposite sides of a very argumentative fence, yet moved during our meeting to the joint position that diverse disease/pest management options are healthy, and they can coexist by establishing localized zones where resident beekeepers can decide together how to collectively manage their colonies.

Vocal anti-pesticide advocates interacted with those concerned about alienating farmers who believe crop production depends on pesticides. The two perspectives established a common ground to work with progressive farmers that encouraged pesticide-reduced options that would benefit bees while sustaining crop production. Commercial beekeepers who operate thousands of colonies and hobby beekeepers with one or two colonies generally attend different meetings. Yet, for the two days of "Bee Audacious" we enjoyed getting to know each other, having meals and socializing, working hard together in breakout groups to generate audacious ideas that a wide range of beekeepers could support.

At "Bee Audacious" we observed that the full spectrum of those interested in bees and pollination could find accord, forming alliances organized enough to have considerable impact on the health and welfare of both managed and wild bees. That common ground covered considerable territory, with a cornucopia of audacious, inspiring and actionable ideas emerging. One set of recommendations focused on habitat protection and enhancement that would benefit honeybees and wild bees alike. For example, government could shift farm subsidies and tax credits to favour sustainable agricultural systems that include pollinator protection as an important component of their management paradigms, and increase conservation easement payments for growers to transform marginal agricultural land into bee-friendly zones.

Habitat enhancements could build on current local, state and federal programs to replant road, power line and rail rights of way, marginal areas in and around farms, and degraded industrial /mining/forestry areas with nectar and pollen-producing plants. Also, mandating stricter regulations around pesticide use, including more extensive testing for pollinator impacts prior to pesticide registration, would dramatically improve pollinator health to the benefit of honeybees, wild bees and the farmers who rely on bees for crop pollination.

Another audacious outcome from our conference was the exciting proposal to create a National Bee Corps across the United States and perhaps internationally, modelled after the Peace Corps. The Bee Corps would enhance extension/ education for beekeepers, from the smallest scale hobbyists to the largest commercial operations. Its core objective would be to formulate and deliver programs that assist current beekeepers while educating the new generation of beekeepers that is expanding dramatically all across the United States and globally.

Another idea emergent at "Bee Audacious" was recognition that, although there have been many anecdotal reports globally about resistant bees, there has yet to be a well-funded, widespread international effort towards selection and breeding for natural resistance. We imagined scaling up research and support teams, connected with beekeepers, to conduct research that selects for colonies with their own built-in defence mechanisms.

Perhaps the most promising idea of all was to build an alliance of interests that could effectively lobby for pollinators. The raw material is there for a robust and powerful lobbying force. There has been a public upwelling of interest and concern around bees, but it has not yet been well organized. Similarly, there are copious organizations with direct or tangential interests in pollinator health, but they have not coalesced into an effective lobby. The Bee Audacious conference was enthusiastic about the creation of a National Pollinator Association, a group under the broadest possible tent that would respect each organization's individual mandates while working collectively to support broad areas of agreement around pollinator policy. Beekeepers, concerned citizens, local food aficionados, wilderness advocates, duck hunters, organic farmers and sustainable grocery chains could all be invited to participate.

"Bee Audacious" provided a powerful lesson in the power of dialogue and diversity to overcome singularity. The varied perspectives at the meeting generated ideas well beyond any individual, just as ecosystems characterized by diversity are more resilient and able to withstand considerably more perturbation than mono-toned habitats. What is true for bees is true for us as well. Pollination systems that employ multiple bee species are far more stable and effective than single-species habitats, just as a beekeeping meeting attended by numerous points of view yielded the most durable outcomes.

Sometimes the most audacious thing we can do is reach across the aisles that separate us to work collaboratively with those with whom we disagree. Disagreements dissolve and cooperation emerges when dialogue rather than debate becomes the modality of interaction. In that way "Bee Audacious" taught us something considerably more important than the pollinator issues that brought us to the Marconi Conference Center. Civility is possible, and positive collaborative outcomes likely, when we rise to respectfully listen to each other above perceived differences.

CRYSTAL CITY

A little bit of everything
just down from the Pentagon

retrofitted, those buildings
converted

apps, speeded up and mobile
workers from DC

that chandelier, totem
from ghost to cool

—drones, up mornings
away and back into

incubator: thousands of square feet
prototypes and monthly fees

across the highway
marketable mergers

just a short walk
from a new Whole Foods.

No one to say the words,
Freedman's Village

no one to mention
that long walk down route one—

SIX-SIDED CELL, WHERE WE FOUND HER—

we saw her then, at dusk or just before dawn
out from her front door, papers dropping—
then later, deepest afternoon, back pocket

tucked into view, folds of four, eight
carried, silent witnesses, and she, striding
street to street, at her throat or 'round her wrist

red coral, a garnet-crusted ring, offerings
to the day's designated god, scented lavender
rosemary-current-golden rod-and-rose-

words roped about her waist, slouched against
shoulders, thin, cotton-draped, linen-embossed
our flight captured in cloth, rubbed three times

pebble, ankh, or cross, round and round stepped
back and forth, the world outside, doors, gates
Look—we wanted to say to her—under your pillow

find us, circling—crouch beside your bed,
palm a pot of bee balm, search bags:
your pencil, pen and paper, your electronic device—

COMPETING DOOMSDAYS

THERE IS A REMARKABLE STORY UNFOLDING IN ONTARIO, QUEBEC AND Minnesota around pesticides and bees, rooted in two competing doomsday scenarios. Grain farmers claim pests will destroy their crops unless they are allowed to use neonicotinoid pesticides, while beekeepers point to an epidemic of honeybee colony mortality that reached 58 percent in Ontario in 2015 and has averaged 35 to 45 percent across the United States each year since 2014, which beekeepers blame on the bee-toxic neonics.

Honeybees and wild bees have been declining globally for well over a decade due to a perfect storm of harmful factors, including agricultural pesticides, massive single-cropped fields of nectar- and pollen-producing plants cleared by weed killers, and a dramatic increase in diseases and pests. Many beekeepers and environmental groups specifically blame the neonicotinoids, so named because of their chemical similarity to nicotine, as the primary cause of diminished pollinator populations. Not surprisingly, pesticide companies claim little or no impact. Today most non-industry experts agree that the neonicotinoids are harmful to pollinators, although the severity of their impact on managed honeybees and wild bees remains a topic of debate, as does the proportion of blame for bee decline that should be attributed to pesticides and to the other factors of pests, diseases, and lack of nectar and pollen sources.

Beekeepers began sounding the alarm about neonics in 1994, shortly after they were introduced, but it's taken over two decades for the scientific community to catch up to their concerns. Indeed, the neonicotinoid saga provides an illuminating example of what works well and what doesn't in the culture of scientific research. We scientists were initially skeptical about the impact of neonicotinoids, because the dose bees were exposed to seemed too low to have impact. Further, there was a more likely culprit for honeybee demise: the varroa mite that was developing resistance to the miticides beekeepers were using in their hives.

French beekeepers noted in 1994 that unusually high numbers of their colonies were dying after being moved into sunflowers for pollination. The sunflower seeds had been soaked with the first commonly used neonicotinoid, imidacloprid, so that when the plant grew it would contain amounts of pesticide toxic to pest insects. Beekeepers speculated that the pesticide was also present in nectar and pollen, and that was what was killing their colonies. But most scientists weren't so sure, since the amount of neonic found in the nectar and pollen was well below the twenty-five to fifty parts per billion calculated to be the minimum dose above which behavioural effects would first appear. Also, seed treatments had elegance to them, since they provided an alternative to spray applications that broadcast pesticides over a wide area, with indiscriminate impact on both pests and beneficial organisms. Elegance has always been attractive to scientists, and neonicotinoid seed treatments seemed to be an advance in pest management that localized pesticides within target plants rather than dispersing them throughout the environment.

Neonicotinoids soon became the highest selling insecticide globally, and reports of honeybee colony deaths coinciding with neonic use proliferated. Still, the earliest field studies failed to directly connect neonic use with colony mortality, and the amount of pesticide in crop nectar and pollen, as well as the amount found in colonies, seemed too low to be the culprit for what came to be called colony collapse disorder. The core barrier for researchers was the toxicology truism "the dose makes the poison," since exposure to neonics didn't seem high enough to be toxic. But then a few scientists began asking whether low doses of many chemicals might be having interactive effects, each harmless on its own but together creating a toxic soup of harmful pesticides.

When neonics were tested together with other pesticides, their toxicity increased dramatically, including neonicotinoids combined with pesticides sprayed by farmers, miticides beekeepers were using in hives and antibiotics commonly applied in colonies. Now there was a clear explanation not only for neonicotinoid impact, but also for synergy between many pesticides that were proving more toxic in combination than would be expected from their individual toxicities. Then wild bee studies kicked in, particularly with bumblebees, and here the results were clear, with neonicotinoids associated with diminished orientation ability and fewer queens produced by colonies at the end of the summer. Most recently, we've learned that neonics move widely outside the crops on which they're used, and the highest pollinator exposures to neonicotinoids often are not from crops but from surrounding vegetation, even at a considerable distance from farms.

Beekeeper instincts turned out to be correct, and scientific opinion has shifted to most non-industry experts believing that neonicotinoids are contributing significantly to pollinator declines. I've come on board to this point of view, but one of my few professional regrets is that early in the neonic wars I relied too much on lack of evidence and not enough on the potential for harm. One of the great strengths of science is to demand data and proof, to rely on facts, yet that can also be our weakness when faced with the need to make scientifically based regulatory decisions before sufficient studies have been conducted. Chemical companies are fond of insisting that regulation should be "science-based," but that's their buzzword for cherry-picking data that support their point of view, usually from research conducted by their own scientists.

One thing we've learned from the neonicotinoid controversy is that the precautionary principle should be invoked by regulators faced with assessing the harmful impacts of novel pesticides on pollinators. Suspected risks and the possibility of harm should be assessed before approval, not decades later after considerable damage has been done. Honeybee research has also taught us that we need more contemporary understanding of the toxicological mantra "the dose makes the poison." This may be true in isolation, but in today's complex toxin-rich environment, the dose of one chemical alone may no longer be a good predictor of its impact.

We've also learned that neonicotinoids are just one of many pesticides contributing to pollinator declines, alongside the non-pesticide issues. The issue with neonics, as with most pesticides, is generally not immediate, catastrophic mortality of honeybee colonies, although those directly toxic events do still occur. It is long-term exposure to what were previously considered non-toxic doses of multiple pesticides that has become ground zero in assessing why pollinators are dying. Insecticides (including neonicotinoids), some fungicides, and the miticides and antibiotics used by beekeepers themselves against mite pests and bacterial diseases have insidious interactive effects at low doses that over time wear down honeybee colonies and weaken wild bees.

It's a perfect catastrophic chemical storm when interwoven with agricultural practices. Low doses of neonicotinoids and other pesticides impact pollinators' immune systems so that bees are less effective at resisting diseases and pests. Many pesticides also interfere with the ability of bees to navigate to and from their nests as well as diminishing their overall activity level. And pesticide exposure also decreases the capacity of bees to detoxify pesticides, thereby increasing their susceptibility.

All of these impacts are occurring in the context of contemporary agriculture, in which pollinators are already weakened by poor nutrition and a growing array of diseases and pests. In this nutrition-poor, disease-rich and chemically intensive farming environment, multiple pesticides formerly considered by regulators to be bee-safe at low doses now appear to be contributing singly and in combination to the gradual decline and mortality of managed honeybees and unmanaged wild bees.

Still, in many jurisdictions the recent impact of neonicotinoids applied to grains has been more immediately and directly toxic due to the application method. The pesticide can be applied in a talcum-like dust used to affix the pesticide onto seeds, but the spray disperses aerially on crops and into nearby habitats during planting. This dust can be lethal to significant numbers of nearby honeybee colonies and likely wild bees as well.

What is remarkable about the neonicotinoid controversy is not the conflict between farmers and beekeepers over pesticide use; that's been going on for over a century. What's unusual is that provincial and state governments are beginning to side with the beekeepers, whose lobbying capacity is challenged compared to groups such as the twenty-eight thousand members of the Grain Farmers of Ontario. Quebec, Ontario and Minnesota have implemented restrictions on neonicotinoids unusual in North American pesticide regulation, with Ontario targeting an 80 percent reduction in neonic use. Farmers in all three jurisdictions can now use only neonicotinoid-treated seeds when they have a serious and independently verified pest problem that cannot be managed by any other means, and then only with the approval of a registered pest management advisor, essentially mandating the desirable but largely unenforced principles of integrated pest management. The European Union banned neonicotinoids completely a number of years ago, and Health Canada is considering banning the first neonic, imidacloprid, across the country.

As fascinating as this story is on its own, it's just a microcosm of the much larger issue of how pesticides and farming are regulated. The mantra of contemporary super-sized agriculture has been that high chemical inputs and vast single-crop acreages are required if we are to feed the world. This assumption is based primarily on self-assured comments by lobbyists representing the corporate agricultural interests that benefit from weak pesticide regulations and strong government subsidies encouraging industrial farming. Until recently, data to confirm or deny these claims has been sparse, although the feed-the-world refrain has become a pervasive mantra driving policy in North America. But recent studies have provided independent research rather than lobbyist-spun information, and the results are clear: organic and sustainable "organic-lite" agriculture are close to or as productive as conventional farming, with greater economic returns to the farmer and considerably less environmental impact.

The question no longer is whether organic and sustainable agriculture are viable from a yield or profit perspective. They are. The questions we should be asking revolve around what levers governments should use to shift farming practices in progressive directions. Loose regulations around pesticides as well as vast subsidies that favour conventional farming have left us awash in annual global chemical use, with about 100 million kilograms (243 million pounds) of pesticides in Canada, 600 million kilograms (1.3 billion pounds) in the United States and 2.7 billion kilograms (6 billion pounds) worldwide.

Stricter pesticide regulations, such as the small but positive steps taken by Ontario, Quebec, Minnesota and the European Union to limit or ban neonicotinoid applications, as well as modifying subsidies to favour a transition towards organic/sustainable practices, would improve farm economics and environmental integrity while maintaining high yields.

Pollinator declines are important in themselves, but more significantly are a symptom of outmoded agricultural practices. Pollinator protection could be the thin edge of the wedge driving agricultural policy towards a sweeter spot where crop yields, farming practices and environmental protection are in better balance.

B. IMPATIENS

Colonies received, one queen, her workers
those foraging abilities, we said,
cloth-i-an-i-din, many times—reduced—

They spoke, sub-lethal, canola fields, seeds,
a series of effects, chemically, and—
colonies received, one queen, her workers
exposure, those doses, pollen consumed

Measured analysis of variance
(ANOVA)-cause mean weights, newly emerged,
complex flowers, the learning rate, assessed
colonies received, one queen, her workers
we hypothesized ANOVA again

B. OCCIDENTALIS

and were obtained, Biobest colony
equipped with a bag containing nectar
five to ten workers, their queen, cardboard-cased

isolated proteins, insecticide
non-GM pollen, transgenic divides
and were obtained, Biobest colony
control Imidacloprid chitinase

pollen traps, cleaned of the dead, frozen packed
all those lost lumps, collected, ground, mixed with
purified powders dissolved, added at—
and were obtained, Biobest colony
and fed the appropriate treatment, twice-
ad libitum, each feeding, fresh old and—

AN ADAPTATION FOR FORAGING

On the hive, we rubbed dragonhead, fennel
to welcome them home—lemon-scented balm
those workers detoxified, intervals—
newly emerged, assayed, not marked with paint
how to get used to it, street choirs sang—
aldrin, dieldrin from Shell and others once

Once, and others, aldrin, dieldrin from Shell
On the hive, we rubbed dragon head, fennel
how to get used it, street choirs sang—
to welcome them home—lemon-scented balm
newly emerged, assayed, not marked with paint
Those workers detoxified, intervals—

Those workers detoxified, intervals—
aldrin, dieldrin from Shell and others once
newly emerged, assayed, not marked with paint
On the hive, we rubbed dragonhead, fennel
to welcome them home—lemon-scented balm
how to get used to it, street choirs sang—

how to get used to it, street choirs sang—
those workers detoxified, intervals—
to welcome them home—lemon-scented balm
aldrin, dieldrin from Shell and others once
On the hive, we rubbed dragonhead, fennel
newly emerged, assayed, not marked with paint

newly emerged, assayed, not marked with paint
how to get used to it, street choirs sang—
On the hive, we rubbed dragonhead, fennel
those workers detoxified, intervals—
aldrin, dieldrin from Shell and others once
to welcome them home—lemon-scented balm

to welcome them home—lemon-scented balm
newly emerged, assayed, not marked with paint
aldrin, dieldrin from Shell and others once
how to get used to it, street choirs sang—
those workers detoxified, intervals—
on the hive, we rubbed dragonhead, fennel

welcoming them home, street choirs sang
newly emerged, detoxified, intervals—
aldrin, dieldrin from Shell, we rubbed dragonhead, fennel

MITES

Mites have been ground zero of colony collapse throughout the world, particularly the varroa mite *Varroa destructor* but preceded by the somewhat less damaging tracheal mite *Acarapis woodi*. The tracheal mite infests the breathing tubes of bees, and popped up seemingly out of nowhere on the Isle of Wight, England in the early 1900s. They were initially devastating to honeybee colonies, but then bees seemed to evolve genetic resistance and the mites became a minor irritant. The mites were then accidentally introduced into the United States in the early 1980s with a similar trajectory: early impact followed by genetic resistance. Most beekeepers no longer monitor for or treat against the tracheal mites.

Varroa was similarly introduced around the globe, often by beekeepers illegally moving bees from one country to another, motivated by rumours that bees from elsewhere were superior to their local honeybees. These mites originated in Asia, where they are a minor pest on other species of honeybee, but have turned out to be devastating to the western honeybee species *Apis mellifera* we're familiar with in North America. The mites feed on pupal and adult bees but more significantly transmit and activate often-lethal viruses. Their destructiveness is well-expressed by their scientific name, *Varroa destructor*.

Chemical treatments for mites require a complex dance on a thin razor: miticides need to kill mites without harming bees or leaving residues in honey and beeswax comb. Ironically, formerly pesticide-averse beekeepers soon found themselves dumping synthetic chemical pesticides into their hives to control varroa. The synthetic miticide strategies have essentially failed because the mites soon develop resistance; the honey and wax become contaminated and these synthetic chemicals have subtle effects on bees that contribute to colony decline.

The holy grail of miticides would be a naturally occurring substance, something effective that beekeepers could point to as compatible with the purity of honey. Everything natural doesn't necessarily fit the bill. Nicotine, for example, is a natural substance evolved by tobacco plants to ward off pest insects, but it's highly toxic to both bees and humans. A synthetic version of nicotine, the neonicotinoids, has been a villain in the ongoing mortality of honeybee colonies all over the world.

There are some natural substances that get better press than nicotine with reputations as organic, healthful substances in human spheres, attractive to researchers seeking compounds that might control varroa. My laboratory and others jumped on this bandwagon early on, interested particularly in neem and thymol as varroa treatments.

Neem comes from the tall neem tree, native to the Indian subcontinent. Folklore attributes quite an array of "anti" benefits from the oil extracted from the tree: antibacterial, antifungal, and antiviral. It's also used as a contraceptive and to combat liver disease, as well as for vague functions like removing toxicants from blood, encouraging healthy hair and as toothpaste. There's been little scientific research into any of these functions for neem, but there is some evidence of neem's limited success as an insecticide, inspiring bee researchers to consider neem to combat the varroa mite and its associated viruses.

Thymol is an extract from the thyme plant, and is the substance that makes thyme popular as a spice. Thymol has strong antimicrobial properties and is an effective fungicide, although its use against mites hadn't been tested before varroa came along.

We focused on neem and thymol because our early laboratory screening tests suggested these might be the best of many natural compounds in combatting varroa without harming bees or leaving residues. We also tested other compounds including citronelle, clove oil, canola oil, grape seed oil and menthol, but preliminary tests found them to be less effective.

The research had two phases. First, we screened compounds by putting about ten mites in a cage with a handful of worker bees, exposing them to the test substance and counting the number of dead mites and bees twenty-four hours later. More promising compounds were then tested in colonies for twenty-four-hour and then longer tests, again assessing the number of dead mites and bees found on mesh screens placed at the bottom of colonies to catch any corpses. The short answer from years of research was that neem has potential but is more difficult to apply effectively, while thymol has proven to be somewhat effective. There are many commercially available, thymol-based products on the market providing options for beekeepers who want to avoid synthetic chemical pesticides.

There's a deeper issue than varroa control, however, one that gets at the heart of how we view our human role as managers of the world around us. Synthetic miticides manifest disturbingly similar patterns: each has nuclear impact when first used, destroying almost every mite in its path and seducing beekeepers into thinking their problem is solved. But soon collateral damage becomes apparent, including mite resistance that renders compounds ineffective and subtle side effects that weaken bees. Varroa rebounds and weakened colonies become more susceptible to diseases and pests, rendering synthetic pesticides as problems rather than solutions.

Naturally occurring substances like thymol have a different trajectory. Beekeepers are slower to adopt because they are only partially effective, and who wouldn't prefer the mite devastation of a nuclear pesticide? But over time the natural treatments have become more popular because, so far, no side effects on bees have emerged and carefully timed applications have reduced, although not eliminated, varroa impact.

Here's the conundrum: do we want to manage the pest problems around us by continually producing atomic options that are initially effective but soon lose their potency, forcing us on a treadmill that can only function if we continually invent new nuclear options? Or, can we accept modest success from control measures that have the advantage of lifelong efficacy and little, if any, collateral damage? It's a simple choice: use lower-key controls and accept moderate pest damage or implement heavy-duty management tools that have short lifespans and deleterious side effects. Too often we choose the bright and shiny technology instead of the less glamorous but longer-term natural workhorse. It's about footprint, and how heavily we choose to tread on the planet that supports us.

O TO BE IN THAT GARDEN

in hexane

Seed kernel, the oil
      the law required, and was called, statutory

Those trees deep rooted
      and were granted and early, instead, the sentence
      under a story

Cold pressed, unformulated
      standard conditions set out, the law, devices, the many

Additional batches
      a suspension, revoked, their faces appeared: laughter

Citronelle, clove
      they removed all images and to symbols they and would and never

Cinnamon
      canola, peanut, grape seed
         menthol crystals
         dissolved, diluted

before the start of the experiment

were conducted
to evaluate
varying concentrations

the years, honeyed and waxed, combed
would dance at night, alone, at least secreted
soft, triple, surface and adjacent

before pouring
          a single disk
obtained from
the minimum
came from, treated with
for control of
stocks of several—

unless specified

syrup, fed, ad libitum
these transcriptions a kind of geometer, alternative sets
taken at two-hour intervals—
violet, sweet nectar—that shade of blue, foraged

again, bio-assays

toxicity of neem to varroa and the bees
these are the only remains
left forewing large, crumpled, obscured
walking the city, after—

Shaking a package of honeybees, photo by Mark Winston.

PACKAGING BEES

THE ROOT OF MYRIAD ENVIRONMENTAL ISSUES CAN BE DISTILLED INTO ONE factor: our failure to balance human ingenuity with the limits of nature's resilience. We are a species resourceful at inventing novel ways to manage and control the world around us. But too often we become foiled by our own cleverness when the problems caused by our cunning become greater than the original issue we were trying to manage.

Beekeepers fit this mould perfectly. Both honeybees and their keepers are highly resilient, able to bounce back from considerable perturbation. Until recently, both were able to handle the slowly increasing level of management we were imposing upon honeybees, but colonies have been crashing and dying for over a decade now, stretched beyond their natural elasticity, no longer able to spring back into shape following manipulation. Simply put, we've gone too far.

Resilience is "the capacity to recover quickly from difficulties; toughness." One classic example of colony resilience and human ingenuity in exploiting that resilience is package bee production. This management system involves shaking bees from colonies into packages that are then shipped thousands of miles to new locations, initiating new colonies or replacing those that died the previous season.

Bees have been shipped for ages, but until modern times they were shipped as intact colonies, usually in woven straw skep hives. The first honeybees arrived in North America in 1622 to Jamestown, Virginia, accompanying colonists on the ocean voyage from England. The bees would have been sealed and kept cool in the dark hold of the ship, surviving the voyage to establish the first colonies of this introduced insect.

Honeybees slowly inhabited North America, moving short distances by colonizing tree cavities as escaped swarms or travelling with settlers longer distances into new territory. Occasionally honeybees made large territorial jumps, shipped through the Panama Canal to the west coast or down American river ways. Commercial beekeeping was well established throughout North America by the late 1800s, facilitated by the invention of standardized wooden hives with movable frames that could be used to expand colonies to grow quickly in the spring. Honey-laden frames could then be removed in the summer and fall to extract the copious honey crops produced by these abnormally large colonies.

The package bee system was another invention that allowed beekeeping to expand its range and commercial success. The concept of shipping bees in packages without comb is credited in 1879 to A.I. Root, founder of a highly successful company that manufactured hives and beekeeping equipment. The industry didn't take off until 1913 when his son E.R. Root developed an improved wire cage for shipping, including a tin of sugar syrup to feed the bees while in transit. The same basic design is still in use today.

The origins of package bees may have depended on technological shipping cage innovations, but the inspiration for this system was biological: swarming. When a colony swarms, about fifteen thousand worker bees leave the nest with the queen and form a cluster under a tree branch or other overhang, often staying for days until scouts have found a new nest site and the swarm moves to colonize their new home. It's not difficult to imagine the eureka moment when Amos Root realized that honeybees could be misled into thinking they were in a swarm by shaking them into a package. And a few decades later, Ernest Root had the inspiration for the wire cage that allowed long-distance shipping of worker bees and a queen, followed by shaking the packaged artificial swarm into a new hive at their destination, which the bees would quickly adopt as their own.

From this simple idea, a huge industry was born that expanded colony numbers across North America. In its prime, a million packages were produced each spring in the warm regions of the southern US and shipped to the northern US and into Canada each spring. The Canadian shipments were particularly interesting; about 350,000 packages were trucked into the prairie provinces of Alberta, Saskatchewan and Manitoba each April. Colonies would grow to huge populations during the long Canadian summer days, routinely producing two hundred to three hundred pounds of honey during the summer, the highest per-colony yields in the world. But then, each fall, colonies were gassed off with cyanide and the empty hives were stored until spring when the next shipments of packages would arrive. Gruesome, yes, but economically profitable; many fortunes were made both by the package producers and the prairie beekeepers. But more than money changed hands; beekeeping families from the north and south frequently united through marriage, creating compelling business and family connections that became a culture in itself.

This system came to a crashing halt over the winter of 1986–87, when Canadian officials closed the border to importations of honeybees from the US because of the varroa mite, a pest introduced from Asia that was becoming widespread but had not yet arrived in Canada. The disruption was extreme and those who depended on packages were furious at the precipitous loss of their most lucrative market.

I was president of the Canadian Association of Professional Apiculturists at the time, Canada's group of researchers, extension agents and regulators. The other members and I received a considerable share of the blame for the border closure, although the most significant driver was the Canadian beekeeping industry itself, which considered the varroa mite more of a threat than the demise of the package industry. Tensions were high; at one meeting in Oregon, a well-known and irate California queen-and-package producer offered to take me outside to the parking lot and settle the dispute once and for all.

Businesses failed, families were separated and illegal importation attempts were frequent. But once again, ingenuity trumped tragedy and Canada's beekeepers responded by exploiting the honeybees' resilience with their own responsiveness. The most widespread innovation that swept across the frigid Canadian prairies was learning how to winter bees indoors. The key, it turned out, was not temperature control. A warehouse full of colonies generates considerable heat, more than enough to counter the below-zero temperatures that characterize Canadian prairie winters that often reach 35°C below zero (30°F below zero) and lower for weeks at a time.

Carbon dioxide turned out to be a more significant issue since respiring colonies generate a considerable amount of CO_2. The solution was to install large fans, sensitive air monitors and backup generators, as well as to keep indoor wintering facilities in the dark under red light, a colour that bees cannot see. Kept that way, colonies persist through the winter from November until April with little difficulty, a tribute to both the honeybee's adaptive abilities and the beekeepers' resilient response to potential ruin.

A second remarkable innovation was the development of methods to ship packaged bees around the world as airfreight from Hawaii, New Zealand and Australia into Canada. Those regions did not have varroa mites at the time, and so the Canadian regulatory authorities agreed to allow packages to be shipped by air into Canada. Again, both beekeepers and bees demonstrated ingenuity and resilience. New package designs were implemented using long, thin tubes that were easier to pack together tightly and provided sufficient ventilation.

Package producers learned early on that shipments needed to be in pressurized cargo holds because the air pressure drops as planes ascend, causing the sugar syrup feeders to explode in unpressurized planes and leaving a cascading torrent of syrup when the cargo holds are opened. Since transit points are necessary for the New Zealand and Australian shipments, packages are taken off one plane, kept cool and dark, and placed on another to complete their flights. Although they come from the other side of the planet, the bees reorient to their new home within a few days of the packages being shaken into hives.

A third response to the border closure was to develop a package bee industry in southwestern British Columbia where the climate is mild enough to shake packages in April and May. My laboratory was integrally involved in this initiative and it turned out to be the most interesting of all as it revealed one of the mechanisms by which honeybees manifest their considerable resilience. The key issue was that shaking packages removes two-thirds of a colony's worker bees into cages, and yet the colonies have not only to survive but thrive to the point of overwintering the following winter and be sufficiently robust the next spring to do it again.

Our studies showed that colonies from which packages have been shaken demonstrate exceptional resilience when given enough time to recover. We removed four, six or eight pounds of bees in mid-April or early May and installed them in packages. By August, those colonies were identical to the control colonies from which no bees were taken in almost every characteristic: brood levels, adult populations, pollen and weight. There also were no differences in honey production from the mid-April shakings, although the May-shook colonies produced less honey, suggesting that May package production had reached the edge of colony resilience to respond to early-season worker loss.

For beekeepers, profits were invariably higher with colonies used to produce both packages and honey compared to those used only for honey production—around $30–35 per colony for controls and $45–55 for the various package shaking options. That was in 1985; profits per colony today are closer to $200–250 per colony. Thus, economically the package bee business in southwestern BC proved feasible, and with today's high level of colony mortality has become an important mechanism for beekeepers to replace winter losses, an industry estimated to have a $20 million potential.

But it's the biology behind package production that's most fascinating. The idea that bees are busy all the time is quickly put to rest when observing colonies through glass-walled hives: many bees spend most of their time standing around, apparently doing nothing. That "nothing," however, turns out to have a powerful adaptive reason behind it. Worker bees from our colonies that produced packages began foraging at younger ages than from control colonies without packages removed, and returned with heavier nectar loads. They also died earlier, with twenty-nine-to-thirty-day average lifespans compared to thirty-three days for controls.

A 2014 study by Paul Tenczar and colleagues at the University of Illinois had a similar result: 20 percent of the bees in their study did 50 percent of the foraging, but when the foragers were removed, the lazier bees in the colonies stepped up and began foraging by the next morning. The function of laziness in the hive seems clear; it's a reserve force, ready to up its game whenever the colony is faced with a crisis or opportunity. Lazier bees live longer, an upside for them personally, but at any point are willing to sacrifice their longevity by working harder, dying younger and turning their work potential into action.

This capacity to keep a workforce in reserve is a powerful adaptation that has been central to honeybee colonies surviving for tens of millions of years. But the complex and interactive set of challenges we're throwing at bees today has been sufficiently severe to overcome even the honeybee's considerable elasticity: depriving them of the diverse pollen sources they need for adequate nutrition, moving them thousands of miles multiple times each year, confronting them with an increasing array of pests and diseases, removing too much of their honey and feeding back corn syrup or other sugars, and exposing colonies to myriad toxic pesticides. Colonies might be able to bounce back from any one or two of those challenges, but excess management and manipulation have tipped the resilience scales beyond the honeybee's capacity to respond.

Those of us who have been with bees for most of our lifetimes are torn. On one hand we celebrate the inventiveness and resourcefulness of beekeepers. On the other we see the depredations our own cleverness has wrought on this remarkable insect. If we were truly ingenious, we would understand that less is more and follow management practices that are within the bounds of honeybee resilience. Until we learn that nature has its limits, we and our attempts to manage the world around us are in for a continued rocky ride.

INDUSTRIAL

from producers in those southern states, they
imported packages, restocked supplies
A. woodi already resulted, dis-

ruptions, the arrival, Africanized
the latter half of April, the first part
from producers, new and lucrative shipments, future quarantines, northern and kept

for the timing, experiments, three packages, shaken, two queens superior—
surplus honey produced, profit "per col"
from producers, now more than double when
sugar syrup, brewer's yeast, litres and
those Canadian dollars deducted.

TO SHAKE THE BEES

- 1 large metal funnel
- 1 wire screen container
- a portable scale

and sampled those workers, test colonies—
queens removed, killed on dry ice

comparisons followed
between treatments
at each sampling time

- Relative abundance
- Relative overall abundance
- Distribution of radiolabel
- Mean amounts of—
- The total numbers and relative abundance

HIBERNACULA

and hid there
for a long time

curled—
thinned

under bark—
rotten stumps

hollow curved
and nested

POETRY OF SCIENCE / SCIENCE-IN-POETRY

SCIENCE, WITH ITS RELIANCE ON DATA AND OBJECTIVITY, MAY SEEM THE least poetic of professions, but scientists and poets have at least one thing in common: we share a love of words and exploration. But science is plagued by jargon, creating a barrier to understanding between scientists and civilians. Still, there is a resonance to the scientific vernacular that is as evocative as poetry. My own field of entomology is replete with insect names derived from Latin that carry historical meaning, and behavioural terms that reveal profound understandings about nature as well as opening the opportunity for contemplation about our human condition.

My own favourite insect scientific name, not surprisingly, is that of the honeybee, *Apis mellifera* L., 1761. *Apis* is Latin for "bee," and *mellifera* translates as "honey-bearing" or "honey-producing," referring to the honeybee habit of collecting nectar and transforming it into copious amounts of honey that allow colonies to survive dearth periods. Every organism has a generic (*Apis*) and a specific (*mellifera*) name, followed by the name of the individual who first described it and the date it was designated. Humans are *Homo sapiens* L. 1758, translated as "wise man," a generous name that we don't always live up to.

The "L" after *mellifera* and *sapiens* refers to Carlos Linnaeus, the Swedish botanist who created binomial nomenclature in the 1700s by which every known organism on Earth is named. Linnaeus has been honoured by the use of just his initial "L," recognizing his seminal role in the naming of organisms, much like Oprah Winfrey has her own magazine recognized by its initial "O."

Apis mellifera L., 1761 is the shortest of poems, but rich with its own cadence, symbolism and array of impressions, emotions, sounds and memories. Recitation of the sparse language in that short name is evocative, standing on its own but richer when viewed through the highly individualized lens of each reader's subjective experience with honeybees.

Another entomological/poetic term that evokes personal resonance is "hibernaculum," a place of abode in which a creature seeks refuge. An insect's hibernaculum is a thin cavity under bark, an underground nest or a curled leaf that provides protection and refuge from predators, winter, rain or other dangerous elements.

I loved teaching entomology and rolling "hibernaculum" off my tongue, a word with its inference of safety and survival, the soft tones of "hiber" followed by the sharp resonance of "naculum." It's such a hopeful word, intimating the most fundamental imperative of all organisms to survive. It's also a very human word. Who hasn't sought to find a safe emotional shelter during difficult periods, to carve out time to rest and reorient before re-engaging with the challenges that confront us?

Another entomological term with literary aspirations is "diapause," referring to a period of suspended development during unfavourable environmental conditions. What rich imagery, the suspension of development's trajectory, with its promise to resume under better circumstances. But there is no guarantee that conditions upon emergence will be welcoming. Tuning to environmental signals indicating when to exit from diapause evolves over thousands of years, connected to historical averages of temperature, rainfall, day length and other factors; survival upon emergence depends on favourable conditions associated with those cues. Changing climate takes a heavy toll on organisms dependent on finding the right food and weather when they leave the state of diapause, only to find that previously reliable cues have become misleading. Many insects are getting the timing wrong during our current era of rapid climate change, with the tragic consequence of being too early or too late to survive.

The word "diapause" also translates into human experience. Buried beneath the word I sense the rhythm of suspension and resumption, pausing or moving forward.

Scientific language becomes poetry for me through the sheer joy of jargon's sound and rhythm, opening doors to meaning beneath sparse words when immersed in their cadence. It is this passion for words and adroit turns of phrase that may unite the seemingly disparate professions of scientist and poet, each seeking language to express those sublime moments of comprehension. In science they are called "eureka moments" from the Greek *heúrēka*, translated as "I have found it"—a recognition of those occasional glimpses underneath the unanswerable questions, vistas that can take our breath away.

NOTES FROM THE MARGIN
(RENÉE SAROJINI)

SO THEN, POETRY AND SCIENCE—BOTH PROCESSES TO MY WAY OF THINK-
ing. And that thinking, always, uneasy with too reified a notion of *the thing* as
opposed to many things, or the making of things, ideas, constructs, each of these
endlessly variable. And in that endless flow of things, we might examine surface
as well as texture and begin to see/sense, within language, notions of "deeper/
sparse" or "excess/absence" or "fullness/lack" and many other such pairings.
These dichotomies perhaps serve as warning: how to know, that's the quest.

Or perhaps, to let go of trying to know anything, or trying to explain, and
just make with the materials at hand. There's delight in reading a scientist explore
poetry; and also, as the poet in collaboration, I'm hesitant—for instance, about
"eureka," about "completion," about "finding." Poetry is a process, language is
material, for many poets. So the idea of "I found it" is more, "I wonder/wander,
lost, full of archive fever, intent on gesture and the incomplete." And this idea of
not finding we find beautifully expressed by John Keats when he formulates that
philosophical entry point, *negative capability*. In a letter dated December 21, 1817
to his brothers George and Thomas, Keats reflects:

*Brown and Dilke walked with me and back from the Christmas pantomime. I had not
a dispute but a disquisition, with Dilke on various subjects; several things dove-tailed
in my mind, and at once it struck me what quality went to form a Man of Achievement, especially in Literature, and which Shakespeare possessed so enormously—
I mean Negative Capability, that is, when a man is capable of being in uncertainties,
mysteries, doubts, without any irritable reaching after fact and reason—*

I've typed out this passage on a Sunday afternoon in August: each keystroke
brings me closer to a poet I admire—the letter found in a compendium published in 1935 and edited by Maurice Buxton Forman, the book found upstairs in
the library collection of my father-in-law, now deceased; a man born in Dublin,

whose passion for literature lasted his lifetime and surely beyond—the papers of the hard-bound book, cream-coloured, ridged, rough-soft to the touch, and musty enough to make me sneeze when I lift page after page—then, pause, and return to Mark's science papers, some of them over forty years old. The way time shifts: memory floats, away from the surface of things. Yes, the more I spend time with this essay about poetry and science, well, who knows what the former is—I should always want, I think, to be in a state of not knowing; and as for science, the more I spend time in Mark's archive, I experience that set of methods and materials, as an invitation to write notes in the margin, questioning everything, performing absence—

Keith Slessor, photo by Mark Winston.

FRAGMENTS

POETRY AND SCIENCE SHARE AT LEAST ONE TRAIT: BUILDING FROM FRAG-
ments. As Renée puts it: "One of my poetry obsessions is the fragment. Each
time I read from my long poems I select fragments, further reducing the pieces,
a reductive process that speaks to me of possibility…"

Scientific research is simultaneously reductive while discovering meaning by
repeatedly recombining small bits of information in different ways. Experiments
resemble poems trimmed down to their simplest bytes, expressing the scientist's
hope that disparate data might assemble into the fullness of story, revealing objective truth considerably more profound than its constituent parts.

So it was that words became a line and eventually a poem as we unravelled
the identity and function of the honeybee queen pheromone over close to two
decades of research. My laboratory, in intimate collaboration with chemistry
colleague Keith Slessor and his students, had become interested in the retinue
of ten to twelve worker bees that surround the queen, licking and touching
their antennae to her furiously for one to two minutes each. Our hypothesis
was that they were picking up the queen's pheromones and transmitting them
throughout the nest. We had made extracts from dead queens to use in identify-
ing her chemical signature, but had no way of determining whether worker bees
responded.

One day, in frustration, one of our students put a dab of extract onto a glass
pipette and thrust it into in to a cage of bees, exclaiming, "Take that, you bloody
bees!" To her surprise, they formed a retinue around the glass as if it were a
queen. We had found our bioassay, but it still took tens of thousands of assays
excising, macerating, extracting, eluting and observing over two decades to
identify nine compounds that work in a synergistic mix, attracting worker bees
to attend their monarch. Each individual pheromone we identified represented
another fragment that then had to be tested in combination with the growing
number of other compounds, until eventually the full poem of the complex
honeybee queen pheromone grew from its nine simple words.

It's a thing of beauty, this multi-fragment queen pheromone, an elixir of elegant function, reminiscent of the elusive perfection captured in the best poetry, where snippets of language weave together into a whole much more compelling than its individual parts. I imagine Renée at work in her writing laboratory, testing combinations of words together, rejecting innumerable linguistic dead ends until the etymological data tell her the poem is done. It's fragments coalescing into meaning at the junction where science and poetry intersect on common ground.

(*In memory of Keith Slessor*)

HONEY FOR THE WINTER

basis of the retinue

includes licking
　　　　signals the presence
　　　　　　　　the social fabric

mandibular gland complex:
　　　　HQMC
none of the known

excised, macerated, extracted
　　　　eluted with mixtures
glass pseudo-queens

　　　were fashioned

cut and sealed
　　　　a small indentation
inserted through a hole

eight-mated queens
　　　　three laying
five received

these queens extracted
in autumn—

bioassay

on occupied frames
containing roughly equal
taken from a colony

the queen, removed
these frames placed
on a sunny warm day

in the centre of the frame
videotaped, analyzed
new sets of five

the colony's own queen
synthetic and natural
the cues—ovary,
and egg laying.

all those layers

slow, inevitable
    benzene, lead
        formaldehyde
        hydro-carbons
            dioxins,
        leached—

honey for the winter

our approach, this study
      genetic life history

Apis mellifera adansonii
Apis mellifera adansonii

with notes, factored
      pollen-feeding, brood-rearing—

Apis mellifera adansonii
Apis mellifera adansonii

First Hives for Humanity honeybee colony, in the garden next to Vancouver's safe injection site, Insite, photo by Hives for Humanity.

Worker honeybees forming a retinue around a glass lure treated with synthetic honeybee queen pheromone, photo by Keith Slessor.

QMP

A CORE MYSTERY AT THE HEART OF ALL SOCIETIES IS EASILY DELINEATED with a simple question: How do thousands, or sometimes millions, of individuals coordinate their activities to work together for the common good? For social insects like the honeybee, the language of royalty we use in describing colony leadership assumes that commands from the monarch, a queen in the case of ants, bees and wasps, control the activities of her many legions of workers. Not quite. The idea of monarchy is too simplistic to describe the underpinnings of the elaborate cooperation that is the signature of social insects.

"Integration" would be a better term based on the elaborate sharing of information that informs workers about the state of their union and guides their decisions about how to best allocate work to serve their colony's needs. For honeybees, the primary information source is chemical, through the queen's pheromones, that profoundly influence the physiology and behaviour of her daughter worker bees. The word pheromone is an amalgamation of the Greek words "to carry" and "to excite," but that translation is a bit of a misnomer for honeybees. The queen pheromone does indeed carry, transmitting information from the queen to the worker bees, but rather than excite it is more of a calming agent, reassuring the workers that all is well and encouraging them to carry on with their duties.

In 1980 I started my faculty position at Simon Fraser University's Biological Sciences Department, intrigued by a letter I had received from SFU chemist Keith Slessor. Keith had considerable experience doing pheromone research on pest insects. He was also a hobby beekeeper and suggested that when I arrived we might want to talk about some collaborative projects involving honeybee pheromones.

As for a bee colony, this type of research requires considerable integration of a wide set of skills, chemists to identify compounds and biologists to test their functions. Our biggest breakthrough, however, was not a result but an approach. We broke down the divide between disciplines and functioned as an integrated team. Chemists learned to dissect out queen glands, and biologists learned to prepare samples for analysis and interpret the complex peaks and valleys that emerged as graphs from gas chromatographs and mass spectrometers. Lab meetings merged our students in free-for-all discussions about next steps, sharing frustrations when things didn't seem to be working and peak moments when a new chemical finally emerged from the soup.

Our second breakthrough was in developing the retinue bioassay by putting fifteen worker bees in a petri dish with a glass lure baited with extracts to determine which chemical regions of the extracts were attractive by the number of bees attending the lure. We then identified potentially active compounds and tested the synthetic versions. This wasn't simple as we were seeking a multi-component pheromone in which a single compound might be inactive alone but quite active in combination with others. The full blend is necessary for the full retinue attraction: remove any one from the blend, and attraction diminishes by 10 to 50 percent. Thus, we had to test tens of thousands of combinations to confirm activity of each component in combination with the others.

We published the first results in 1988, a five-component blend we called Queen Mandibular Pheromone (QMP) since the entire blend was secreted from the queen's mandibular glands. QMP included previously identified components (E)-9-keto-decenoic acid (9ODA) and two forms of (E)-9-hydroxy-2-decenoic acid (9HDA), and two new compounds present in smaller amounts than the others but critical for the pheromone's activity, 4-hydroxy-3-methoxy-phenylenthanol (HVA) and methyl p-hydroxybenzoate (HOB).

We went with that for a while, but knew we were missing some of the pieces. Chris Keeling, a graduate student of Keith's, subsequently discovered four more, some from the mandibular gland but two from elsewhere in the queen: methyl oleate, coniferyl alcohol, cetyl alcohol and α-linolenic acid. There are at least one or two more to be identified as we're still not quite up to the level of complete substitution for the queen.

Now that we had a fuller pheromone blend, we could explore more effectively how the information contained in the blend was dispersed in the nest. The queen only encounters a small number of a colony's twenty thousand to fifty thousand workers each day, so there had to be some means of information transfer that alerted bees throughout the colony that the queen was alive and healthy.

We discovered a breathtaking elegance to the transmission system, again through a unique interdisciplinary collaboration. One of my students, Ken Naumann, worked with Glenn Prestwich, a chemist then at Stony Brook University in New York. Glenn is difficult to categorize, but can perhaps be best framed as a medicinal chemist with a talent for discovering therapeutic biomaterials and founding startup companies, but who also has an interest in insect pheromones.

I first met Glenn during the tail end of my tropical biology days when he and I were teaching in an Organization for Tropical Studies course in Costa Rica. Glenn, like Keith, had compiled a considerable body of work with insects, and his skill as a chemical ecologist brought him to the attention of the course organizers. But Glenn had another claim to fame that became a legend among tropical biologists. La Selva, a research station in Costa Rica, has a network of tree canopy platforms that researchers can climb up to and rappel down when done. Glenn finished his work in the canopy one day and jumped backward off the platform thinking he was attached to the rappel line. He wasn't. He fell about two hundred feet, his fall slowed only because one of his arms had got wrapped around the rope. Miraculously, he got up after his fall and walked away, although his arm is marred with a fabulous rope-burn scar.

Besides falling out of trees, Glenn and his colleague Francis Webster had attached a radioactive label to 9ODA so that its movement could be followed through the nest. Ken Naumann treated queens or lures with the labelled phero-mone, picked out workers that had just contacted the queen or lure, washed various body parts and put the washes through a radiolabel detector to deter-mine how much pheromone was where on the workers' bodies. Then he allowed workers that had contacted the queen or a lure to move through the nest, and again captured and washed workers who were contacted by the former reti-nue bees. He continued the chain serially, following the passage of pheromone through the nest. Finally, he did whole-colony experiments to determine how the pheromone dispersed at the hive level. What emerged was a clear picture of not only how pheromones moved through the nest, but also how worker bees deleted pheromone from the colony, which turned out to be a critical aspect of how the queen's message was perceived.

We learned that there are two types of retinue-attending bees who pass on the queen's message, which we named "licking" or "antennating" messengers, de-pending on whether they only brushed their antennae over the queen to groom pheromone from her body or also licked her with their long tongues and stroked her with their forelegs. The licking bees pick up considerably more pheromone, but both types then move through the nest contacting other workers and pass-ing the queen's message to the receiving bees, again with their tongues, antennae and forelegs. The recipients go on to do the same with gradually diminishing amounts of pheromone in each exchange.

This messenger system explains how worker bees know the queen is present without most of them ever contacting her. But how would they know if the queen was gone? Astute beekeepers notice that worker bees begin behaving nervously within about fifteen minutes after removing the queen, suggesting that there must be a mechanism for the colony to quickly cleanse its palate of pheromone and recognize the queen's absence.

Removal of pheromone from the system is as important as distribution, and here again bees provide an elegant example of how nature solves tough problems. Any pheromone transferred between workers is quickly perceived but then rendered ineffective by making its way internally, either migrating through the bee's external skeleton or being groomed and then swallowed. The internalized pheromone may have some profound physiological effects on worker bees, but the nature of its internal activity after absorption, if any, has yet to be determined.

Thus, a honeybee colony integrates the activities of tens of thousands of worker bees through communication. The constant exchange of chemical information between workers is important, but just as critical is removing pheromone so that information is current. The workers remain open to incoming information, ready to change their behaviours quickly in the face of new facts.

Our research followed the same pattern, intensely sharing information between our biology and chemistry laboratories to guide daily decisions about how to best allocate our time and effort. Communication was key; each day we optimistically designed an experiment in the morning, conducted it in early afternoon and gathered late in the day to pore over the data. Our long-term success was dependent upon being open to incoming information from each day's experiments, modifying our approach quickly in the face of data informing us that, yet again, we were on the wrong track.

Usually what seemed like a brilliant hypothesis early in the morning turned out to be a blind alley by the afternoon. Occasionally, the data we graphed late each day formed into a configuration telling us we were experiencing the rarest of scientific events: a discovery. Weeks would go by without a breakthrough, often months, but then there were moments when some aspect of the honeybee's chemical world would emerge, sharp and clear.

Those moments were ecstasy: data yielding insights about the hidden underlay beneath the surface, the glue fastening thousands of individuals into a socially cohesive community.

SCENT, HER MESSAGE—

calling, *9-O-D-A, 9-O-D-A*
pulsed, steady and smooth
five blended, secreted
mandibular, those glands
washed those chains

serially, snared through the nest
calling, *9-O-D-A, 9-O-D-A*
those afternoons, dusk also desire
licked, stroked, tongue and foreleg
a glass lure

that rope, a long way down
scarred forever, calling, *9-O-D-A*—

HER LOVELY FACE

pheromone deposited on the comb
small colony workers, those honeybees
in a garden of such delight, the queen—

in a garden of such delight, the queen—
to collect nectar, more into pollen
pheromone deposited on the comb

pheromone deposited on the comb
the total effort into foraging
in a garden of such delight, the queen—

in a garden of such delight, the queen—
unfolding, those seasons cycle, hills climbed
pheromone deposited on the comb

pheromone deposited on the comb
by sudden events such as predation
in a garden of such delight, the queen—

workers, that patch of flowers, depleted
we called them *Apis mellifera*
pheromone deposited on the comb
in a garden of such delight, the queen—

QUEENRIGHT

"QUEENRIGHT" IS A BIT OF JARGON I LOVE FROM THE WORLD OF BEEKEEP-
ing; an optimistic word indicating that the queen is present and the colony tran-
quil. Workers are going about their tasks in an organized manner: the young are
being reared, nectar and pollen processed and the entrance well-guarded from
external threats.

"Queen loss," on the other hand, is colony tragedy writ large. Honeybee
workers recognize that the queen is present by her pheromones, the magic glue
that turns tens of thousands of individuals into a colony. Her pheromones are
picked up by the retinue workers who surround the queen, then move through
the nest and pass the blend to other workers. In that way, the queen's presence is
communicated to the colony and the diverse functions of the pheromones that
influence worker behaviour and physiology are spread through the nest.

Workers begin responding to her loss almost immediately due to pheromone
levels in the colony diminishing; the workers must begin rearing a new queen
quickly or the colony will not survive her passing. New queens are reared from
young worker larvae by feeding them a special nutritious meal of royal jelly. If
queen rearing doesn't commence within a few hours after the queen dies, the
worker larvae will become too old to switch their developmental pathways towards queens.

We beekeepers also have jargon we use should the rearing of a new queen
fail: "hopelessly queenless," a phrase of deep despair. The disheartened worker bees soon become highly aggressive toward each other and any unfortunate
beekeeper who might open their nest. The colony spirals downward into social
chaos, inexorably dwindling until it perishes.

We share with honeybees the tragedy of chaos when events upend the peace-
ful order of our own well-functioning societies. Heartbreak erupts periodically
around the globe as previously coherent societies become, well, hopelessly and
tragically all too human.

AND HER WORKERS

nous avons examiné le facteurs
we examined the factors

Apis mellifera L., Queenless
those [　] at different ages
the young, their in-nest tasks

cleaning cells, rearing brood
older foragers who guarded

newly emerged, only to become
a queenless colony, also we compared
that were caged for days, the number
         fourteen

allowed to consume pollen, royal jelly—
our findings suggested: sugar syrup, wax foundation
         screens passable—impassable

from each cage, we extracted—
frozen and stored

AFTER THE REMOVAL

at the start of each test, caged, and then, and—
shaken from colonies into wire
clustering, mesh packages, a caged queen
fed 2:1, a solution, sugar-
syrup, left overnight, morning and we
placed her—caged queen on a wooden cross
plastic covered, slotted, workers released
hung, four swarms weighted, set thirty metres
apart. Each day tested, caged, removed, and—
glass dishes, ether evaporated
studies have shown, there appeared to be, and—
unanswered questions, workers following—
at the start of each test, those caged queens removed, each day, apart, the queen tested, she—

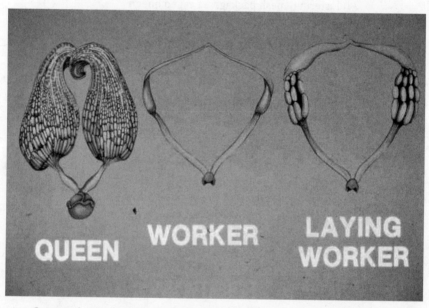

Ovaries of queens, workers and laying workers, drawing by Elizabeth Carefoot.

THE POETRY OF METHODOLOGY

SCIENCE CAN PROCEED ONLY AS QUICKLY AS THE MATERIALS AND METHODS allow. Often, there is a question we would love to answer through research, but the procedures have not yet caught up to the question. So it was with worker bee ovaries.

Darwin himself recognized the lack of honeybee worker reproduction as a potential deal-breaker for his theory of evolution by natural selection. Worker bees have ovaries, but they fail to produce eggs in the presence of the queen, so the workers sacrifice their own reproductive potential for that of their monarch. This degree of reproductive sacrifice shouldn't happen as the driving force behind evolution is the powerful impulse to replicate your own genes through reproduction.

Many theories have been proposed to explain why workers sacrifice their egg-laying for that of the queen, but the simplest is that they have no choice. That is, the queen is preventing the workers from reproducing. We and others conducted research demonstrating that the honeybee queen's mandibular pheromone (QMP) prevents workers from developing egg laying abilities, but at the time we were studying this phenomenon, the scientific tools were not yet available to answer the key question of *how?*

We could only approach the edges of this research by asking the tangential and ultimately unsatisfying mechanistic questions to define the parameters that influenced, but didn't determine, worker ovary development. To do so we isolated bees in cages, dissected and measured their ovaries and bled bees to determine the amount of vitellogenin, the protein that becomes egg yolk, in their blood. Our methods involved incubating, sampling, incisions, capillary tubes, bleeding, freezing, staining and scanning—all long-established tools of the scientist's trade, but also evocative words that attract a poet's scrutiny.

We found that young bees are most likely to develop ovaries, being well fed matters and measuring egg yolk protein in the blood of adult workers is correlated with ovary development. But now, almost twenty years later, a group in New

Zealand has managed to address the core question we never had the methodology to approach: how does QMP prevent worker ovaries from developing? Their research methods went far beyond our crude incision, bleed, stain and scan; today's state-of-the-art research includes *in situ* hybridization, immunohistochemistry and quantitative RT-PCR, among other melodious but intimidating nomenclature for contemporary scientific analysis.

Their results, hidden beneath the erudite language of science, lie at the core of understanding social evolution. The Notch signalling system is used in many animals to initiate egg development, but in honeybees its function has been reversed to inhibit egg development. Exposure to queen pheromone suppresses the production and deposition of egg yolk protein in workers, whereas the absence of the queen and her pheromone frees workers of her influence and allows a protein to be produced that leads worker eggs to develop. It's a system as complex as the language used to describe the researchers' methodology, but its outcome is simple and essential to the social structure of honeybee colonies. No pheromone? Inhibition is removed, yolk is deposited and egg-laying starts.

If the queen disappears, the societal order she imposes through her pheromones breaks down and chaos reigns. Young workers liberated from the queen's control quickly develop ovaries and lay eggs, although colonies are doomed to disintegrate within a month or two because these unfertilized worker eggs can only mature into male drones. The last weeks of a queenless colony's life are tragic, characterized by dwindling worker numbers and intense fighting in what had previously been a placid and cooperative social unit.

The ovary story revealed much about the evolution of social insects, but also uncovered a dilemma at the intersection of science and poetry. The rhythm of the words and terminologies around scientific methodology can easily roll off the poet's pen in appreciation of the language, but without the reader easily understanding the scientific story they tell. For scientists, deep understanding of the language is vital, yet we can lose sight of the compelling tale beneath the data.

Hiving a swarm of Africanized bees, French Guiana, 1977, photo by Robin Henschel.

GLASS PSEUDO-QUEENS

residuals tipped,
deposited down
            within a cage
            those honeybees
circular holes
disposal plastic

            cut, sealed, both ends
            a small indentation
on evaporation of the solvent
within the area of the pseudo-queen
            around her to touch—lick

            lick, touch, their antennae—
head-first to the glass, their antennae
            their pseudo-queen
            her presence detected
                        the licking of the lure
                        raised in the late summer

            and between colonies on the same day
framed overnight, those workers emerged, marked

            we painted enamel, dots on the thorax
and returned to the parent colony

o sing to us, of—
wooden cages used for micropipettes

IN THE COURT OF THE HONEYBEE QUEEN

an-   te-n-   nae to—
li-ck, groom, feed—

                    surrounded
        fluc-   tu-   ating, first workers, then spread
                    sem- i- o- chem- i- cal

            [o sing to us, كيمياء]

a blend of five compounds
        QMP-QMP-QMP-QMP-QMP

to elicit retinue
        to attract swarms
                to stimulate pollen foraging
                        to calm queen-less workers

from super-sisters to half-sisters,
to li-ck, groom, feed—

An-   d those colonies where—

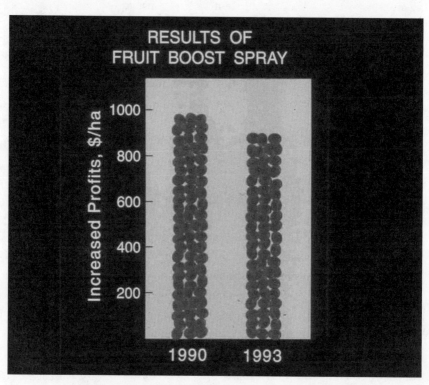

Profits from spraying blueberry with honey bee queen pheromone
formulated as Fruit Boost, drawing by Elizabeth Carefoot.

BLUEBERRY

HERE'S WHAT WE KNOW: HIGHBUSH BLUEBERRY IS SERIOUSLY UNDER-POL-linated, with yields 10 to 20 percent lower than optimal, costing growers in my home province of British Columbia alone about twenty million dollars annually. Crop pollination is the primary economic benefit of bees. Bees don't pollinate some crops such as wheat and corn that are wind-pollinated, but most tree fruit, berry and oilseed crops require or benefit from bee pollination, as do many vegetables. Bees collect pollen as their only protein source, accumulating pollen grains on their hairy legs and bodies while visiting floral stamens, which then fertilize seeds when the pollen is transferred as worker bees forage between flowers.

Pollination is a particularly big deal for blueberries, which have multiple seeds and require about twenty bee visits per flower to be fully pollinated. Fewer visits result in small, misshapen berries that reduce both yield and grower profit. Ideally, bumblebees would be carrying out the pollination tasks because they buzz flowers to dislodge pollen, which is more effective at transferring pollen than honeybees' more passive visits. But there are too few wild bumblebees in and around blueberry fields because of heavy pesticide use and weed killers that destroy the wild flowers upon which bees depend when blueberry isn't blooming. There are another hundred or so species of wild solitary bees that could also be pollinating blueberries but have been similarly decimated by agricultural practices. Thus, many growers rent honeybees at the high price of $100–150 per colony, although others save money by hoping their neighbours' honeybees will fly into their fields.

Early in my career, I leaned towards technology as the solution to this under-pollination problem. We had identified five components of the honeybee queen's pheromone in 1988 and nicknamed it "QMP" for Queen Mandibular Pheromone, since all the components known at that time were produced in her mandibular glands. Because it is highly attractive to honeybees, we imagined that spraying it on blooming crops might encourage bee foraging and thereby improve pollination, increasing yields and ultimately profits to growers. QMP dissolves easily in water, so we were able to spray it on selected crops that require bee pollination, but like blueberry, were under-pollinated. Included in our list were kiwifruit, pear, blueberry and cranberry, but not apples, since apples are generally over-pollinated and have to be thinned by growers to produce fewer but larger, sweeter fruit.

We set up test plots and used backpack sprayers, tractor-pulled air-blast sprayers or a helicopter in the case of cranberries to disperse the pheromone once the crops had reached sufficient bloom. We had no idea what dose of QMP would work, if any, so we tested doses of zero (control: water spray only) up to extremely high, ten thousand queen equivalents per hectare, with one queen equivalent being the amount of pheromone we estimated a queen produced in a day. Also, since field conditions in agriculture can be enormously variable site to site and year to year, we conducted tests over two or three seasons, and at multiple locations each season. The results far outstripped our modest expectations. The increase in numbers of foraging bees on the various plots was substantial, often 40 to 50 percent higher on sprayed than unsprayed.

Yields were also higher in sprayed plots measured by either number of fruit or weight, with increases in the proportion of larger, more profitable fruits. The economic outcomes were even more impressive. When all costs were deducted, profit to growers increased by $950 per hectare for blueberries, $1,200 per hectare for pears, $4,204 per hectare for kiwifruit and $4,252 per hectare for cranberry. These are stunning results and piqued our curiosity as to why the queen pheromone, which has no known function in the field for foraging bees, would increase foraging and crop yields.

When faced with an intriguing finding, the best strategy is to put your best student on the case, and I was fortunate that Heather Higo, the woman who ran my lab, became interested in pursuing a master's degree and was excited to work on this project. Heather did field studies in blueberry and cranberry first and discovered that foraging honeybees in sprayed plots visited more flowers and stayed in plots longer than in unsprayed plots. Each bee visited more flowers per trip, which translates into better pollen movement, enhanced pollination and higher yields, particularly in crops that require more than one bee visit to set the most and largest fruit.

She then did studies at sugar syrup feeders placed a few hundred metres from glass-walled research hives at which we could observe returning foragers, spraying the feeders with low or high doses of QMP or a water control spray. Foraging bees that discovered the feeders returned to their colonies and performed the waggle dance, recruiting hive-mates to forage and providing information about the distance and direction to the newly discovered resource.

Recruitment was higher to the pheromone-sprayed feeders. Returning foragers unloaded their sugar cargo faster and returned to the feeders sooner, similar to studies that found short turnaround times in the hive and faster buildup of recruits when nectar is perceived as higher value. Presumably there's something about the vigour and intensity of the dance, more energetic movements, higher frequency buzzing while dancing, an elevated temperature of the dancing bee, or some other factor that excites the follower bees to leave the hive and visit the QMP-sprayed crop. The precise stimulus is still to be determined, but its effect is to increase foraging and improve pollination.

There was one aspect of Heather's study that puzzled us. She saw no increase in recruitment or forager dancing at the high dose, similar to our field studies that also found no increases in foragers or yield at the highest dose. We observed a similar phenomenon in colony studies testing whether low or high doses of queen pheromone would inhibit swarming, finding that the low dose was effective but not the high dose. Perhaps the workers' sensory system has a threshold beyond which QMP is not effective or in some way confuses the bees when exceeded too far beyond the dose experienced from a single queen.

Taken together, the crop and recruitment experiments demonstrated that QMP could increase yield and profit on crops that require bee pollination. It works through higher numbers of bee visits due to enhanced recruitment, more time spent in fields and more floral visits per trip when foragers encounter the appropriate dose of QMP. We licensed QMP to a small Canadian company that marketed it as Fruit Boost to enhance pollination. It was a successful product for many years, but the company went bankrupt in 2015 for reasons unrelated to Fruit Boost and it's no longer commercially available.

As much as I enjoyed the challenge and success of invention, something about Fruit Boost has always nagged at me: why should it be necessary? I was challenged by invention, but Fruit Boost was a product solving a problem that shouldn't exist. If we had smaller, more diverse crop plantings rotated and interspersed with more natural habitat, we wouldn't need to artificially enhance pollination because there would be sufficient wild bees to accomplish that critical task.

Our default human position to invent something to manage a problem isn't always the best impulse. More products equal more cost to growers, and often create their own problems that then need to be managed by yet another clever invention. Pesticides are another example: overused because the way we do agriculture encourages pests beyond ecosystems' natural resilience by which predators, parasites and diseases keep pests in balance.

The ecological services that could be provided by bumblebees and other wild bee species would be a more elegant and effective solution to pollination management, relying on billions of successful years of evolution instead of the short and often destructive history of human ingenuity. Reduce insecticides, stop spraying so much weed killer and diversify plantings on and around farms—wild bees would thrive and products like Fruit Boost would be rendered unnecessary.

It's an odd position to take, advising against my own invention in favour of nature's expertise, but using inexpensive ecological tools seems like a better long-term strategy than continuing to invent costly products. The best way to boost fruit production is not to go forward, but to revive the healthy ecosystems of the past for the benefit of both humans and honeybees.

AT PLAY IN THE FIELDS OF THE QUEEN

Apis mellifera L.,
        queen who would secrete
glands mandibular
        to turn to touch her face
        antennae—to lick
her body connected—mandible by a duct

Queen, as found by—those intervals

10	(0)
9	(0)
8	(0)
3	(2)
4	(2)
5	(0)
1	(1)
2	(1)
6	(1)
4	(0)

A CONTINUUM

i.

sugar, syrup, wax foundation
royal jelly—pollen in honey

eight full-sized colonies,
newly emerged

as drawn flame
tumblers—

the wells empty,
then full

cut grass,
a nest, papery grey

tucked string, unknotted
at the gate, a swing

to and fro—flung out
frames sealed, brood without—

were chosen, random, mixed,
—caged—

ii.

pollen, entrance to the hives
traps, dried, ground powder
royal jelly equal, the honey
Plexiglas, again the cage
a set of removable doors
attached to each, wax [   ]

incision, measured in the briefest
micro-millimetres, the dorsal cuticle
—all about them that summer, the [   ]
abdomen, capillary, gel and dye
stained, de-stained, scanned
       intensities

that was, there was, frozen, stored
disturbed, constricted, newly emerged
incubated, sampled, examined,
we took our time, and classified
to pass foot to, and again, in cages
tested, and with—

sugar, syrup, pollen, royal jelly
          in honey
             with mixtures, and caged
the influence of the Age
found between
               differences—

APPLES AND HONEY

SEPTEMBER AND OCTOBER ARE IMPORTANT MONTHS FOR HONEYBEES AND beekeepers, their final opportunity to bring in the last dribs and drabs of fall honey, and ours to prepare hives for the long winter ahead. But fall beekeeping and winter colony survival are dependent on spring bloom because it's those nectar-producing flowers of spring from which we harvest honey in the fall, and it's the honey we leave for the honeybees each fall on which they survive until the next spring.

The Jewish new year, Rosh Hashanah, also happens in September or early October, a festival of renewal and reflection where bees and honey play a prominent role. We dip slices of apple into honey and recite, "May it be your will, lord our God and God of our ancestors, to renew this year for us with sweetness and happiness." The simple rhythm of blessing, dipping and merging apple and honey holistically unites my own disparate identities of beekeeper, scientist, teacher, writer and Jew. It is at these moments that I feel most whole, and at these times of celebration that I most deeply understand the role of bees in nature and in my own life.

Apples would not exist were it not for the pollinating influence of the bees, which transfer pollen between flowers every spring, setting the seed for the apple fruit. The apples, for their part, produce sweet nectar in their flowers, which attracts the bees to dip their tongues deep into the flower, knocking pollen off the flower and onto their hairy bodies in the process. The pollen rubs off on subsequent floral visits, fertilizing the flowers and the growth of the new apple fruit begins. The nectar from the apple flowers is carried back to the bees' nest, turned into honey and stored for the winter, providing honeybee colonies with food to survive until the next spring when the cycle is renewed as the bees pollinate again.

We celebrate this annual cycle by joining the apple and honey together to renew the sweetness of the seasons. This closely intertwined relationship has deeper meaning because the quality of the apple depends on the number of bee visits. The more bees that visit each flower, the larger and rounder the fruit. The quality of the fruit is further enhanced when the donor and recipient trees are different varieties, yet another celebration of diversity's inherent value.

Quality also has to do with the diversity of bee species that visit the blossoms, with many dozens of wild species attending to apple pollination in addition to the managed honeybees. Each bee species works the flower differently, transferring pollen in various ways and thereby contributing their own unique style to the critical task of pollination.

It is similar with human societies: it's through the cross-fertilization of ideas and talents that we express our best communal selves. We derive strength and wisdom from our mutual visions, just as the apples are improved by the visits of diverse bees to set fruit.

The feel and smell of the bee yard are there with me during our holiday celebrations, connected with the cycles of the seasons and the profound beliefs and history from which my own rituals descend and my descendants will learn from and enjoy. Yes, there is much that can be revealed when the taste of crunchy apple is mixed with the sweetness of honey. But isn't it always like that, with wonder all around us when we open our eyes to the profound insights imbedded in the simplest of pleasures?

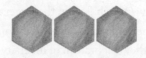

THE BEEKEEPER'S LAMENT

#1 amounts (ng) of 9-ODA

bee visits to flowers
    abundance assessed

    an area below
    and bloom,
        a presence

those field conditions
    ten minutes, that interval

    bumblebees, and honey
    foragers and counted

competition: the honeybee,
    the natives
repeated at five locations

and counted, berry crops
far natural vegetation

blueberry
cranberry

raspberry
          les abeilles pollinisatrices—
sauvages ont été prelevées

#2 *found body, surface of*

thirty-eight solitary bee species
collected, nine berry crops
near natural and far—

dialictus, most common
three species, *Andrena*
bombini most abundant

both crop and natural
Bombus mixtus Cresson
Bombus terricola Kirby

o cranberry, blueberry, raspberry
o capture and rated—direct
observation

#3 *mated, those queens after*

low diversity, striking
when compared with
that natural, those collections

low bush blueberry
the Fraser Valley
in the year of the reign 1982

forty-eight species of bees
collected on natural vegetation
fifteen species on all three berry crops

GONE BUT NOT FORGOTTEN

I'VE LEARNED QUITE A BIT FROM BEES, LESSONS AROUND THE VALUE OF collaboration, clear communication, a strong work ethic and social responsibility. But I've learned as much from the people I met through the bees as I did from the bees themselves.

My first encounter when I moved to BC in 1980 was John Corner, the Provincial Apiarist from 1950 to 1983. John was born in Ladysmith, a small town in BC built around the logging industry. His family soon moved to the remote Kootenay Mountains where he grew up hiking and canoeing in the surrounding wilderness.

John began his lifelong interest in bees as a twelve-year-old working for a local beekeeper. His passion for bees continued to develop during the Second World War while fighting in Belgium. He was a decorated hero, receiving the Order of the British Empire for gallantry, but rarely discussed his combat experiences. He did often mention that he studied beekeeping as a distraction from the war around him, developing a habit of reading voraciously that he continued throughout his life. John had no formal education beyond high school, yet was one of the most educated and scholarly individuals I've known. Self-taught, he became an expert in Aboriginal rock paintings, consulted by experts worldwide about the BC pictographs that he meticulously documented. His book *Pictographs (Indian Rock Paintings) in the Interior of British Columbia* remains a classic and much-cited work, detailing hundreds of pictographs that he recorded over decades of travel throughout the province.

His impact on beekeeping in British Columbia was immense, a major factor in expanding what had been a hobby and sideline endeavour into a commercial industry. Most notably, he conceived and led a project to breed queen bees for BC, collaborating with esteemed researchers globally to design and implement the project. Honeybees have an odd genetic system and breeding bees is one of the more difficult tasks in animal husbandry, yet John and his team studied the subject intensively and worked through the complex genetics to produce reliable lines of bees. Those queens were among the best I've seen and many of the individuals working on the project became commercial breeders still influential in the BC beekeeping scene.

John Corner kindly took me under his wing when I first arrived in British Columbia. I was equipped with a fair bit of academic knowledge but little experience relating to beekeepers. We travelled the province together for many years, visiting individual beekeepers and attending meetings, providing a unique opportunity for me to observe and learn from John about how to interact with often-quirky beekeepers. John was the quintessential gentleman, as gracious when chatting with servers in the many small-town restaurants at which we shared meals as he was talking with dignitaries. He was an appreciator, curious about the lives and stories of everyone he met. He had mastered the art of being quiet but attentive, sparse in responding but resonating with thoughtfulness and kindness when he did.

John's listening skills made him an insightful judge of people, but he wasn't judgmental, just perceptive. This skill yielded excellent choices in those he hired, sometimes after just chatting for a few minutes, and many of the individuals he mentored are still leading figures in beekeeping. I don't recall John ever directly instructing me, or anyone else, about how to be, but I know I absorbed important lessons through spending time in his orbit. I came to appreciate the power of listening, the importance of curiosity and the value in building relationships with those from different backgrounds and perspectives than my own. The beekeeping world served up a rich source of friends and colleagues, largely because I followed John Corner's example.

He also inspired me to apply the thoroughness of basic academic research to applied questions. John's approach to bee research combined extensive combing of literature, careful listening to the practical experiences of beekeepers, meticulous experimental design, a high regard for replication through large sample sizes and conducting experiments over multiple years and in diverse locales. Our research on package bees, pollination, swarm prevention, pest management and other practical research topics in my laboratory benefited greatly from John's example. Due in a large part to his influence, my laboratory became known for our careful attention to practical problems.

Cam Jay, a professor at the University of Manitoba, also became a close friend and an important role model. He, too, was the most careful of researchers, equally esteemed by the research community and beekeepers, but what he taught me by example was that work was not the primary goal of existence.

Cam developed a pursuit that gave him precious time alone but also provided opportunities to visit with his many friends across the prairies. He was a pilot who loved to fly, rebuilding a 1949 airplane that he kept in a hangar on property he owned outside of Winnipeg with a grass runway. He had quite a reputation for swooping down and landing unannounced at beekeepers' homes, on whatever pasture could serve as a landing site. He'd drop in, visit for a bit, and then head off to another unexpected stop. He was particularly renowned for winter flying, when he would land on a frozen lake populated by ice fishing cabins, knock on a door with an empty pizza box he kept in his cockpit, and ask the fishermen whether someone there had ordered a pizza. He was invariably invited in for a chat, a drink and some fishing time before taking off to fly back home.

Cam was a kid at heart, hardworking but also fun-loving. His home was covered with photos of special family events, friends and travels, but it was only in his home office that his numerous awards, plaques and honours were displayed. He told me once that he kept them privately rather than at his university office because he didn't want people to think more highly of him just because he had received some awards.

One of my great regrets is that I never had the chance to fly with Cam, but we did have two other traditions. I mentioned to him once that I was a serious pie aficionado, and from that day on there was always a fresh pie waiting for my Winnipeg visits, baked by his wife Doreen. Cam was reserved about many things but his love for Doreen was highly public. He was known as the "Billboard Romeo" in Winnipeg because every ten years, around their wedding anniversary, he purchased a large billboard advertisement to proclaim his lasting devotion.

I saw Cam often at conferences, where we exercised our second tradition. We'd sneak away from meetings to seek out the best local milkshake, as shakes were almost as compelling for Cam as flying. The pies at home and the milkshakes away were mostly a convenient excuse to talk, and here I benefited from Cam's considerable wisdom about how to live a life. There was much contentment in Cam's life, but also sorrow, as there is for all of us. His infectious laugh provided a wonderful lesson that, as difficult as life can be, it can also be replete with joy and love.

Like John Corner he was never too obvious with direct advice, but nevertheless would provide gentle caution when he saw that perhaps I was taking myself too seriously. Academia is a profession in which overwork is rampant, and ego abounds. I so valued Cam's example of a different work-life balance than I saw in many of my colleagues, and learned from our time together that there were things in life more important than the job. Work hard but always with a sense of fun, love your family and enjoy your friends—these were the core guiding lights for Cam, messages that I very much needed to hear as a young faculty member tempted to overwork.

Eva Crane was the opposite of both John and Cam, although close friends with them both. She was direct with advice where they were roundabout, pointed where they were subtle. Our first encounter was more of a wrestling match without a referee than a small talk getting-to-know-you session. Eva was quintessentially British, and in looks and demeanour could easily have doubled for the Queen. Born in 1912, she earned a Ph.D. in nuclear physics in 1941, an unusual achievement for a woman of her era. She married shortly after, and she and her husband were given a beehive as a wedding present to supplement their Second World War sugar ration.

Her passion for bees soon won out over nuclear physics, and in 1949 she abandoned that career and started an organization that eventually became the International Bee Research Association. In that capacity she edited their journals, wrote 180 articles and many voluminous, comprehensive and seminal books about honey, beekeeping and the archaeology of bees, mostly while in her seventies and eighties. One of her books, on the rock art of honey hunters, reflected a joint interest in pictographs she shared with John Corner.

Our first meeting was in my office at Simon Fraser University shortly after I'd arrived in 1980, and it turned into a tussle, albeit an enjoyable one. We'd barely said hello when she insisted that we find a larger room with a long table at which to work. She was carrying a manuscript I had submitted to the publication she edited, the *Journal of Apicultural Research*, and she didn't want to waste a moment before getting down to fixing my writing errors. We got to work and spent most of an afternoon reading through the manuscript word by word, arguing over what I thought were the most minor of changes. At first I was taken aback, then perhaps a bit defensive, but by the end of the day I had to admit how much I'd enjoyed myself.

Eva was my first serious editor, and through her I came to appreciate the importance of exact language and the power of focus in writing. Words mattered to Eva, not only in themselves but because bees matter, and anything that matters deserves the most rigorous attention to the highest standards of precision, clarity and nuance that language can provide.

John, Cam and Eva all passed away within three years of each other: Eva in 2007, Cam in 2008 and John in 2010. I felt the loss of each of them deeply, partly because they represented a rich era in bee science and beekeeping, but also because each had graced me with models for how I, too, might grow. From John Corner I learned to listen and to treasure the great diversity in personalities and attitudes revealed when we approach others with curiosity rather than judgment. Through Cam I grew to be a more balanced person, becoming more focused and effective at work as I learned to relax at home. Eva reminded me of the thrill in a well-turned phrase and the joy in finding just the right words (but not too many), igniting a passion for language that is still among my greatest delights.

As I age I am beginning to understand that a common phrase we use for those who have passed on is more than just a cliché. John, Cam and Eva: for me, you may be gone but you are truly not forgotten.

À MOISHE (TO MARK)

spring's bloom, fat summer, fall's harvest
apples to honey, when October ends, begins
that portal, opening, dip, recite, if not for
that transfer, set the seed, swell the gourd,
nectar sucked, a hairy-backed bee
what if our fingers, stroke, or rub, carry over
to visit, that flight, the dance and stored for winter
a number of, the more—
rounder, varietal, species named, unnamed,
destroyed, remembered, into the bee yard
you brought me—and so we whispered
let the song reside in us forever

UNSEALED

we came then to the entrance, bathed threshold
water and smoke, those names, laid down, streamed stars

night-watch, hidden, fled to never-never—
in their bush, fragrant blooms, thyme, penstemon

opened—a single lotus, carved white cup
where sat the queen, her emanations sent

this were the morning, after tears, longing—
that song: purple vibrations, edged harvest

hyacinth, borage, lilacs, lavender
arrival, that company of, farewell

deep caves, waves of sand, tidal pools moon-lit
that Douglas fir, cones dropped, chipped apart, held

and saw again all whom we loved: shining
surfaces inscribed, thousands, light webs, lifted—

Renée Sarojini Saklikar in bee garden, Central Park, Burnaby, BC, photo by A. Dix.

BEES IN THE CITY

COMMON SENSE SUGGESTS THAT WILD BEES AND HONEYBEES WOULD DO poorly in cities. After all, a quick look at urban habitats reveals a preponderance of asphalt and concrete devoid of blooming crops and degraded by air and water pollution.

Except common sense has turned out to be wrong. Most cities are oases of bee diversity and beekeeping. Many municipalities host considerably more wild bees and healthier managed honeybee colonies than in nearby natural or agricultural settings. My home city of Vancouver is on the low end, with fifty-six wild bee species, not because we're a degraded habitat but because we're located in a wet coastal climate not particularly hospitable to bees. Berlin is the wild bee diversity champion, with 262 species, followed closely by New York with a bit over two hundred.

Bees are emblematic of the many little-noticed small organisms upon which ecosystems rely. Wild bees do well in cities because they thrive in the in-between, folding themselves precisely into interstitial habitat cracks. They inhabit small patches of sandy soil, cedar chips or hard dirt, former rodent nests or hollow twigs and stems, and shop for food at nectar- and pollen-producing flowers growing in empty lots, road and rail rights-of-way, backyard gardens, parks and even sidewalk cracks.

Cities may be disturbed habitats compared to pristine nature, but they do have one quality that supports high bee diversity and abundance, and that's the varied nature of cityscapes. Diversity begets diversity, and a close look at cities reveals myriad small but highly varied micro-ecosystems. In this way, cities express the holy grail of conservation, to maintain the biodiversity so critical to the health of all ecosystems. Cities turn out to be a most hospitable bee home for just that reason, because a considerable natural diversity remains in between the man-made.

It seems ironic that in the face of global bee collapse the best news stories are emerging from our cities. Bee City, USA, for example, is "making the world safe for pollinators one city at a time." It's a remarkably simple organization that encourages cities to apply for a "Bee City" designation, which depends on their adopting simple policies and programs that favour the health of wild bees and managed honeybees. Successful applicants commit to sustaining pollinator habitats by reducing pesticides, extensively planting bee-friendly flowers appropriate to local climates, passing bylaws that allow beekeeping and initiating pollinator gardens where the public can learn about and celebrate local bees. The original Bee City was Asheville, North Carolina in 2012.

The program has since expanded to sixty-two US and seventeen Canadian cities, as well as thirty-one university campuses. Bee City includes large municipalities such as Seattle, San Francisco and Toronto, and smaller towns including Gillette, Wyoming, Gold Hill, Oregon and Chestermere, Alberta, and even a US military installation, Wright-Patterson Air Force Base. Bee City and many other initiatives indicate how citizen interest from the ground up can be an effective force for environmental health. Supporting bees in cities has become a global movement, building from the local to the national and even international levels, and it's making a difference. Awareness and concern about bees has never been higher, in large part due to urban residents whose inspired advocacy has yielded positive municipal outcomes for urban bee health.

Bee-friendly organizations have wisely built a tent large enough to accommodate beekeepers as well as wild bee enthusiasts. Managed honeybees do as well in cities as wild bees do, for the same reasons: diverse flowers blooming throughout the spring, summer and fall that produce a continuous supply of nectar and pollen and reduced or no pesticide use. Urban beekeeping has exploded over the last decade or so, expanding due to public concern about bees and as a by-product of mounting interest in growing food within cities.

The bee enthusiast world isn't conflict-free, however. There are a few voices in this community that would like to exclude honeybees from cities, arguing that their presence overwhelms feral bee populations by out-competing them for flowers. The potential is certainly there if thousands of honeybee colonies were to be concentrated in a small area, but urban beekeeping tends to the small and backyard, with but a handful of colonies within flying distance of each other. So long as beekeeping remains a backyard urban hobby, managed honeybees are unlikely to have much negative impact on other bees, and there is a great advantage to having beekeepers as allies for wild bee preservation. Beekeepers tend to be organized, vocal and effective in advocating for honeybee-friendly policies, and what supports honeybees will be similarly supportive for wild bees.

There is much to learn from the presence of bees in cities beginning with how the wild and the managed can coexist, a lesson that contemporary agriculture would be well served to heed. The key, of course, is balance: recognizing that ecosystems can withstand gentle management but soon become stressed when our human hand becomes too heavy. Oddly, farmers have much to learn from urbanites about how agriculture could become more sustainable. Urban bees are a prime example of how ecological services thrive when balance is paramount.

Agriculture today is highly distorted from a bee's perspective, with pesticide use so heavy and terrain disruption so extensive that few wild bees survive. As a result, massive numbers of honeybee colonies must be rented and brought in temporarily when crops are blooming to compensate for the lack of wild bees. It's a common tension between the natural and the managed. The status quo for bees in cities is healthier than it is out on our farms, ironically because cities might seem to be more intensively managed habitats than farms. Perhaps not— there may be considerably wilder habitats in cities than in cropland, at least the kind of wild that results in biodiversity and robust bee populations.

We will know that agriculture is improving when farm habitats become as hospitable for bees as cities. Farmers would be well served to study the "wilding" that cities manifest, and consider how to create those in-between zones and chemically reduced ecosystems that would be more hospitable to bees. We'll know they've been successful when we see farms healthy enough to sustain sufficient wild bee populations so that fewer rented honeybee colonies are needed for crop pollination.

There's another issue that's percolated through the bee friendly community, one that at times has riven conservation movements particularly in North America, where so many of our plants have been accidentally or deliberately imported. What is "native"? What is "wild"? What should we be conserving? Purists say we should encourage only native plants and dismiss plantings of introduced species, even if their flowers produce voluminous quantities of nectar or pollen. The traditionalist's rationale is that endemic plants best support native bees, some of which have co-evolved highly specific pollinating relationships with those plants. Less doctrinaire bee enthusiasts are happy to foster any high-yielding nectar or pollen-producing plant, whether native or introduced, wild or managed. This cadre recognizes that humans have irrevocably altered habitats since our earliest emergence as a species, and what seems introduced today will eventually become native as we become accustomed to its presence.

We humans have an unparalleled capacity to terraform our surroundings to our own specifications. We can choose to support ecologies that provide beneficial services such as wild bees, or create bee deserts that require importing managed bees to take the place of the natural. We can be purists about endemic versus imported, or manifest flexibility in supporting ecosystems that mix the old and the new. We can split off into adversarial, rigid positions that divide, or seek balance and conciliation through which a wide array of perspectives can find a home.

If bees in cities have taught us anything, it's this: we, like nature, thrive when diversity blooms. The small and often unnoticed can be powerful healers of fractured habitats. As bees do for nature, so the daily work of many unheralded urban residents creates the healthiest communities in which we express our best human traits.

Indigenous rock painting, photo by Renée Sarojini Saklikar.

NOTES FROM THE MARGIN

of no fixed address

Dear [   ] and [   ]:

that time with you—upcountry, driving roads, rip-rapped
those spaces, markings on stone, walls and [   ]—

STRATHCONA

the way of and found—

strathcona, they chanted to remember,
colony farm kitsilano community gardens
u-b-c botanical queen elizabeth vandusen—

> the honey and the mason bee, large un-mowed patches
> narrow corridors, a mix of high and low, residential
> old-growth forest, a diversity of soil, cedar chip, sandy and gravel

global-positioning-system coordinates: [   ]
mixed fruit, berries, flowers and vegetables

> *Allium* sp., *Lavandula* sp., *Centaurea* sp., *Vicia*—
> *Solanum tuberosum, Rubus discolour, Origanum* sp.,

garden plots surrounded

shrubby areas—herbs, those flowers, longed for

backyard, that park, those flower beds—

> *Myosotis sp., Prunus sp., Solanum tuberosum,*
> *Echinacea sp., Lupinus sp., Salvia sp.*

o, sing of—

the river coquitlam and that lake where
            numerous wood stumps—
railway tracks high density and industrial

deer lake u-b-c main library queens park
            como lake green links
jericho beach gastown railroads

            cariboo heights roadside cariboo avalon
            that ranch park powerline
those traditional sites—backyards—blue mountain

            surrounded by and frequently—

letters left behind, hidden

bee species
captured by

sweep netting
urban backyards

gardens, parks
powerline corridors
      road edges

sing: *Andrena, Bombus*
Dialictus, Megachile—

repeatedly, and observed—

at the great gate called destruction

flowerbeds, backyards
a total of fifty-six bee species
wild and abundant, late spring
honeybees, the end of summer

Apis mellifera, managed
Bombus flavifrons Cresson, wild
cotoneaster and blackberry
buttercup and foxglove

dandelions, all their visitors
to maintain the bloom
salmonberry, oregano, fireweed
weeping, we collected names—

that moment in battle when—

weedy patches, May to June
        as then was called
bumblebees collected wax, glossy leaves

cherry laurel: a number of shrubs
        the city, where there might be—
we walked the perimeter, not realizing

micro/macro, richness, abundance
wild bees peaking in late spring
as then was called

in synchrony, he whispered
those battered, bruised, outside
specific and fragments and hosting

A. angustitarsata, rare
Bombus occidentalis Greene, decline
and recalled—

we walked valleys to riverbeds
        date consistent with outside
butterflies, also—

and wandered, those community gardens
        as once were called—

Mark Winston conducting workshop at Hastings Garden, Vancouver, 2015,
photo by Hives for Humanity.

HIVES FOR HUMANITY

URBAN RENEWAL HAS TAKEN ON MANY FORMS ACROSS THE GLOBE AS CITIES struggle to reinvigorate decayed neighbourhoods. The outcomes are sadly predictable: first cheap rentals and low property prices attract hip businesses and a few trendy young home renovators, followed by more organized developers assisted by friendly municipal zoning. A decade or so later the urban remodelling is complete, and the former impoverished residents and marginal businesses have been displaced to the next down-and-out neighbourhood.

Vancouver's Downtown Eastside (DTES) was just such a neighbourhood awaiting gentrification, known for decades and still recognized as Canada's poorest postal code. The DTES used to be Vancouver's classy shopping district, with its prime location adjacent to downtown, but the big department stores slowly moved uptown, and in their place came concentrated social housing, soup kitchens, shelters and an extensive suite of government and non-profit services for the impoverished. The inevitable redevelopment began about a decade ago, initiated at the edges of the DTES and gradually spreading its tendrils deeper inside. Many from outside the area were surprised when residents put up unexpectedly strong resistance to the encroaching gentrification. "Community" emerged as the operative word, and organizing turned out to be an effective counterbalance to development.

The municipal government responded to the unexpected neighbourhood pressure and implemented an official plan to build an extensive range of social and low-rent housing, accompanied by appropriate social, business and medical services, to ensure that the less prosperous residents of the DTES could remain in their community. "Unexpected" is the right word because more prosperous Vancouver residents had trouble understanding that a neighbourhood deeply afflicted by poverty, homelessness and mental health and addiction issues might also be a community. Those from away saw the DTES in its most limited parameter, as "a group of people living in the same place," without understanding that the definition of "community" can be considerably more expansive.

I've worked at Simon Fraser University's downtown campus at the edge of the DTES for the last fifteen years, and rented an apartment in the neighbourhood for three years during the period when redevelopment was a rampant issue. It was bees, though, that drew me into a deeper relationship with the neighbourhood, through the organization Hives for Humanity, a remarkable example of how the community of bees can serve as a coalescing point for a community of people. Hives for Humanity (H4H) is a non-profit organization that encourages community connections through bees, fostering human interactions with nature while contributing to a local sustainable economy and supporting at-risk populations of people and pollinators. As they put it on their website, "The bees are an incredible equalizer, they demand your focus and your respect, and they teach us how to give those things to ourselves and each other, regardless of whether you are coming from plenty or scarcity, from calm or from chaos, or from anywhere on the spectrum in between."

My intersection with H4H and bees in this unlikely environment began when I interviewed one of its founders, Sarah Common, and a few H4H participants for my book *Bee Time*. I was impressed, and soon became an informal advisor to the group as well as taking a role every summer conducting workshops in the neighbourhood about bee biology. H4H keeps up to a hundred colonies of bees in and around the DTES, on rooftops or in some of the remarkable urban farms that have popped up on vacant spaces in the neighbourhood. The farms themselves produce healthy food for the community, most of which is sold cheaply or donated, and the bees are an integral part of what has become a significant food resource. My neighbourhood bee sessions are held outdoors in the Hastings Garden, a large empty lot at the edge of the gentrified zone that is awaiting development as a social housing site but used for now to intensely grow everything from lettuce to raspberries. And, H4H keeps a handful of colonies there, around which we gather each summer to talk about interesting aspects of bee biology.

When the weather cooperates, we stand around an open hive and talk as the bees are flying in and out. Occasionally it's raining and we leave the hive closed and talk underneath a set of tarps and umbrellas. Either way, I think of our gathering as a circle of curiosity. Individuals trickle in from the street, each slowing down from the frantic pace of the streets as they join the circle, becoming engaged and fascinated by everything bee. Bees become the common denominator, attracting people from a full range of incomes, cultures and histories. Yes, there are a few of the new gentry who have moved into the neighbourhood with stable homes and comfortable incomes. Others have histories that speak of fractured lives and street experience. It is rare for the homeless and indigent, and the prosperous and well-housed, to come into such proximity, yet there they are, in a circle, from disparate lives but united by curiosity about bees.

Our afternoon programs begin simply with the call-and-response of their questions and my answers, but soon move into stories, perhaps their memories of bees kept by an uncle on the farm, or a moment of joy in the midst of urban chaos watching a bee buzz a flower for pollen, slowing the frenetic pace of the DTES for just a moment. To sense, to touch, to talk, to smell and to stroke is how community is built, one connection at a time. Sitting around the hive, each question and comment trades information that grows intimacy through sharing understandings. Nature's marvels surface through past experiences, but as we talk there is also a palpable deepening of that magical and elusive essence of community.

We've talked about how a bee visually slices nature into its constituent parts using its compound eyes, a mosaic of six thousand tiny lenses, each of which sees only the smallest piece of the visual picture. Each miniscule image is summed together in the bee's brain to form a composite, much like disparate personalities merging together into a community, with considerably more richness together than any one alone.

The honeybee dance language is another community-building topic of discussion—the remarkable system whereby one scout bee finds a flower and returns to the hive to communicate its distance, direction and quality, thereby recruiting a squadron of workers to visit the site and collect nectar and/or pollen. The bees' system is simple: distance is communicated by the time spent buzzing in the dance, direction by the angle on the comb relative to the sun outside the colony and quality by the vigour of the dance.

Our circle of interest notes the uncanny similarities between the honeybee dance language and how the DTES community passes around information that might be important to residents. The word on the street too often involves heartache rather than resources, perhaps a wave of drug overdoses due to contaminated street drugs or construction of a new upscale housing project or business. Still, while dancing to flowers and communicating street information may seem worlds apart, they both represent the same critical aspect of community: the importance of information transfer creating collective action from individual insights.

The subject of dance language dialects emerged at our most recent gathering, particularly fascinating since around the circle were many dialects of language and experience. Honeybees from different parts of the world have evolved subtly different vernaculars. For example, bees from one region in Europe might buzz dance for three seconds to indicate flowers eight hundred metres away, while an African bee might buzz for two and a half seconds to indicate the same distance. Interestingly, a bee placed into a colony with a different dialect will initially be confused, but will soon learn the new language and accurately fly out the correct distance.

The Hives for Humanity participants represent a hodgepodge of dialects with a rich array of accents, ethnicities, religions and histories. Many have undergone profoundly difficult challenges in their lives, some with mental health issues, others with addictions and many afflicted by extreme poverty. Some are still immersed in these challenges while others are healing; some are quite impoverished while others have comfortable incomes and housing, yet all share the common vernacular of curiosity about bees, and through learning about bees, an interest in learning about each other.

Finding that shared dialect about bees opens the door for the making of plans with futures that hold the potential for community rather than isolation. These are simple conversations with the potential to weave together a caring community. When we leave our program, neighbours who might not otherwise interact have planted the first seed of a relationship. Perhaps no more than, "Hi, how are you?" will result next time they meet on the street, but those are the first tenuous bonds from which communities grow and strengthen. Perhaps they will meet again at an H4H event, volunteering to plant nectar and pollen plants or build hives. Perhaps a spontaneous coffee date will emerge, or working together on a community issue or bonding over that first taste of the new season's honey.

There is one other bee biology topic that comes up frequently, resonating with the profound power of community. Each foraging bee collects only a tiny amount of nectar from flowers, then returning it to the hive to be processed by house bees. These younger workers take the nectar from foragers and transfer it to cells, adding enzymes and capping the cells with wax, all to transform the floral nectar into the nutritious and long-lasting honey. Each micro-drop of nectar adds up, until after a season the colony, working together, has stored many hundreds of pounds of honey.

This is the lesson of the bees, exemplified through H4H: we too can build healthy communities when we work together with purpose, the ineffable wonder of being part of something more than just our isolated selves.

NOTES FROM THE MARGIN

401 Main Street
traditional, ancestral, un/ceded

Dear Paul at the *Carnegie Newsletter*,

All these years we've been and—

still faithful,
still un/invited, on these territories—

Sincerely,

[   ]

HOME IS WHERE WE START FROM

antennae to sense
      touch-talk
      smell-stroke
together—constant—six thousand
compounded lenses to form
      lines, dis-
      -rup-tions—that mosaic, or, undercurrent, edge-
movement, with violet
      emissions, calling:
tell us, o sun
      wave after wave
this light,   light place
      where clouds will come
queen, to form around—
      ten is a number
        and twelve, every part, body to
stroke, nine chemicals
      touch-lick-lick-touch
all our messages—*quick now, here now*
      before and after
      sudden in a shaft
      blended those five
      compounds, mandibular
glands to signal, wave after wave—
to lay eggs and surround
      wave after wave—

LISTENING TO THE BEES

MANY OF OUR MEMORIES ARE SINGULAR EVENTS, BUT OTHERS REPRESENT accumulated incidents, sometimes dozens or hundreds of repeated moments merging into one recollection.

That's how I remember the Swarm Team walking into apiaries to collect data, as one event repeated during a lifetime of fieldwork. There was a similarity to each trip, a portal opening our capacity to listen to the bees beyond the immediate details of the research we were conducting.

We first had one, then a pair of pickup trucks, crew-cab size, to carry a contingent of students and assistants out to our apiary sites. These were often early morning runs because the data we needed to collect required us to go through colonies before foraging workers started to fly. We'd meet at the lab before dawn, someone bringing doughnuts from the nearby twenty-four-hour Tim Horton's. The trucks had been packed with our gear the afternoon before to save time, and we'd set out to the Fraser Valley where we kept most of our colonies.

Apiary sites tend to be down farm roads or rutted dirt tracks, often requiring a short walk beyond where even a four-wheel drive pickup can reach. We'd pack in smokers, veils, bee suits, hive tools and any equipment we needed to mark bees, measure colonies or collect samples.

Whatever the purpose of our visit, those moments of settling into the apiary to work remain visceral. I can still smell the burlap burning in our smokers, feel the cool early morning air, see that pre-dawn first light of day and hear the quick buzzing of the bees as we cracked the lid of the first hive.

What is most striking after decades of those data runs is how these repetitive experiences gradually merged into revelations more expansive than the data we were collecting. Visit after visit, year after year, I absorbed an unconscious empathy for the communal life in the hive and an understanding of the close relationships between bees and the flowers they forage on and pollinate.

These perceptions became ingrained in a manner that amplified the research we were conducting, but the strictures of science leave little room for speculating about underlying perceptions that carry us beyond data into the unmeasurable. That's the conundrum of science: we feel that we need to separate data from emotion, yet factual analysis and spiritual understandings are both integral elements of the human experience. We certainly produced new findings about bees that stood up to strict scientific scrutiny, yet like our colleagues we kept the numeric and spiritual poles separate, revealing only the data through our research papers and at scientific meetings. It's not that we scientists are personally cold and devoid of feelings—far from it. Rather, it's the culture of science that puts up a firewall between data and belief, driving us to edit out the personal in favour of the technical.

Our research utilized the scientific method, posing hypotheses and designing tightly focused experiments, but information doesn't necessarily equate with listening, and doesn't mean we *hear*. There are meaningful depths to be plumbed if we couple the modern practice of science with the ancient musings pioneered by the natural philosophers, expanding from data to encompass cultural, social, philosophical and spiritual insights.

There are many paths into the riches of that world, but for me collaborating with Renée and her poetry has deepened my own thinking about the science I've done over the last forty-five years. I was surprised when Renée expressed interest in obtaining some of my old research papers, which I had mostly forgotten but she saw as a motherlode of inspiration and language.

Her interest stimulated me to take a closer look. The papers themselves are written with the typically unreadable jargon and density of academic research papers. Yet, there is poetry beneath the stilted style, emotion when stepping back from the minute details of experiments and attending to the broader implications. I wish that scientific journals were structured so that research articles were followed by a connected essay or poem, fulfilling the potential of science to be both experimentally meticulous and personally reflective. *Listening to the Bees* has been an attempt to expand our research by attending to that more contemplative dimension.

Bees are ideal vehicles with which to layer in a reflective component to the more controlled environment of science. Perhaps the most personally expansive outcome surfacing from our studies has been understanding how innumerable individual actions coalesce into community with overall impact much greater than the sum of separate acts. Insect colonies such as honeybees express the tension between private achievement and communal success that is at the heart of being social. We humans, of course, seek personal gratification to an extent likely unknown to a bee, but one lesson to be gleaned from their model of communal commitment is that the greatest satisfaction may come not from private gain but from providing public service to our communities.

Collaboration became another theme of our research that has flavoured my perspective. We examined how bees work together with common purpose to efficiently allocate work within the hive, as well as shifting the colony's attention from growth into the complex behaviours of swarming. Perhaps revealing the remarkable capacity of honeybees to integrate colony needs into work assignments was a sufficient outcome, but in writing this book I also became aware of a more personal impact of these scientific studies.

The Swarm Team developed a culture influenced by the very studies we were conducting. Our working model mimicked that of the hive, with leadership as a loose organizing factor but otherwise based on decentralized decision making as each student relied on the others for advice and assistance during heavy work times. Regular meetings to exchange information and allocate work encouraged a cooperative mindset, and the seasonality of each project allowed us to shift and focus resources throughout the year.

Another element we absorbed by spending time with bees is the intense nature of their communication. Honeybee workers inexorably listen to each other on many channels, particularly chemical but also visual, auditory, vibratory, gustatory and likely other modes we may not yet recognize. We became most familiar with the chemical channel. Decades of observing worker bees incessantly exchanging pheromones eventually became a metaphor for how our own societal cohesion is similarly dependent on continual exchange. Experiencing the precision with which bees communicate, the nuances of their various languages and the effort they apply to interaction certainly influenced my motivation to write for and speak to non-scientific audiences, and the value I place on clarity.

Another set of our research results revealed a key aspect of personal and communal resilience: rest. Bees have a reputation as busy, and while they are remarkably focused when working, they also are surprisingly relaxed when not on duty. Our studies revealed that one function of that rest is to provide a reserve of work and energy that could be called on when needed. We exalt the workaholic, especially in academia, but understanding the connection between down time and resilience in honeybees is a powerful tool to direct our own work habits. Following the bees' model, I rarely work evenings and weekends, and am renowned around the office for my short naps every afternoon after lunch.

Interspersed throughout our work on honeybees were studies of the diversity and abundance of wild bees in urban and agricultural habitats, as well as their value as crop pollinators. This work underscores a vital message that we too often ignore by favouring the technological advances of product-oriented science over the environmental concerns expressed by another scientific faction: ecologists. The decline of wild bees, and our concomitant dependence on managed honeybees for crop pollination, provide powerful evidence about the current imbalance between industry and environment. I increasingly came to see even our own work using queen pheromone to attract honeybees to crops as favouring products over ecological services. In recent years, listening to the wild bees has inspired me to be a vocal advocate of reducing pesticide use and diversifying crop production with the hope we can enhance wild bee populations to become our go-to commercial pollinators.

It has been a rich journey spending so much time in apiaries with scientific inquiry as the framework through which to exercise curiosity. I've truly enjoyed the science, the discipline of data, the joy of results driving the never-ending next sets of questions, the camaraderie of students and the thrill of discovering something not previously known.

It is in the transcendent concordance with another species, the layer beneath the data, where the bees' greatest gifts may lie. Listening to the bees connects us to the ineffable mysteries we will never resolve or fully understand. As a scientist, I find it satisfying that data and studies can only take us so far, that there is a realm where there are no answers, only wonder at how little we can know.

Even now, when my beekeeping and research days are over, I often find myself returning to the bees in mind and memory. Dawn is breaking, we're in the apiary, the smokers are lit, veils are on, hive tools in hand. It's that electric moment of expectation at the threshold of once again listening to the bees.

We open the lid of the first hive—

AND THE DANCE MOST OF ALL

these bees have dialects, they said
a dance-language, distance-flowers

vibrational, these honeybees' tune—
scent, touch, taste, hum—straight run circle

their dance, these honeybees, the shape
straight, run, circle, vibrational tune

the shape of a figure eight, dance
scent, touch, taste, hum—these honeybees—

APPENDIX: THE SCIENCE

Mouthparts of the Long-tongued Bees: The twenty thousand or more species of bees in the world are quite diverse but essentially divide into two groups: those with long tongues and those with short tongues. Tongue length is functionally critical as it determines which flowers bees are able to visit for their nectar. Bee tongues and associated mouthparts are intricate, a complexity useful to taxonomists trying to determine how the various species of bees are related. I studied the fine anatomical details of this labiomaxillary complex and used these structures to determine evolutionary relationships between long-tongued bees (another student studied the shorter-tongued). The study revealed a few structures not previously described, and contributed to organizing the taxonomy and evolution of bees. It also had an exciting spinoff result suggesting that highly social behaviour in bees had arisen not once, which had been the previous scientific truth, but twice. Highly social behaviour is rare in the animal kingdom, and any instance of its independent evolution is a notable and exciting scientific discovery.

Winston, M.L. and C.D. Michener. "Dual Origin of Highly Social Behavior Among Bees." *Proceedings of the National Academy of Sciences of the United States of America,* no. 74 (1977): 1134–37.

Winston, M.L. "The Labiomaxillary Complex of the Long-tongued Bees: A Comparative Study." *University of Kansas Science Bulletin,* no. 51 (1979): 631–67.

Stingless Bees: How bees manipulate pollen has been of great interest to entomologists as a tool to probe the evolution and taxonomic relationships of bees. The most defining characteristic of bees is that they have plumose hairs with which they groom pollen from flowers and pack it onto specialized structures on their legs or abdomens to carry this protein-rich food back to their nests. In this study, we examined behaviours and structures associated with pollen collection among all the bees, but were particularly interested in a remarkable group of tropical bees with the surprising characteristic of having lost functional stings over evolutionary time: the Melopinini. Stingless bees seem to be superficially similar to honeybees, but close examination of how they move pollen from flower to nest revealed some differences that spurred us to examine whether these two highly social groups of bees were perhaps dissimilar in other traits.

Michener, C.D., M.L. Winston and R. Jander. "Pollen Manipulation and Related Activities and Structures in the Apidae." *University of Kansas Science Bulletin*, no. 51 (1978): 575–601.

Winston, M.L. and C.D. Michener. "Dual Origin of Highly Social Behavior Among Bees." *Proceedings of the National Academy of Sciences of the United States of America*, no. 74 (1977): 1134–37.

Cross-fostered: Cross-fostering compares attributes of individuals raised in parental environments to those raised in foreign situations, allowing researchers to tease out the relative importance of genetics and environment. We compared African honeybees and European honeybees and subspecies that originated in either Africa or Europe but were imported into the new environment of South America. The subspecies showed genetic differences in their own colonies, but individuals responded strongly to the environment of the colony they were placed in. That is, colony environment trumped genetic background, so that nurture dominated nature.

Winston, M.L. and S.J. Katz. "Longevity of Cross-fostered Honey Bee Workers (*Apis mellifera*) of European and Africanized Races." *Canadian Journal of Zoology*, no. 59 (1981): 1571–75.

Winston, M.L. and S.J. Katz. 1982. "Foraging Differences between Cross-fostered Honeybee Workers (*Apis mellifera*) of European and Africanized races." *Behavioral Ecology and Sociobiology*, no. 10 (1982): 125–29.

Party Piece: Demography is the study of how births, deaths and reproduction contribute to population growth or decline. It's most commonly used to build life tables with which insurance companies set rates, government develops policy and industry predicts consumer trends. The same tools can be used to study animals, and for honeybees provide insights into how colonies grow and eventually split to reproduce by swarming. I studied colony demography of African bees introduced to South America as part of my Ph.D. dissertation, asking the question: "Do individual worker lifespans change as colonies grow, and if so does that contribute to the ability of the African bees to swarm at high and unprecedented rates compared to European bees?"

Winston, Mark L. "Intra-colony Demography and Reproductive Rate of the African-ized Honey Bee in South America." *Behavioral Ecology and Sociobiology*, no. 4 (1979):279–92.

Swarming: We studied honeybee reproduction by swarming in many habitats, including tropical South American jungles, colder temperate Kansas prairies and the rainy coastal environment of British Columbia, Canada. Decades of research revealed a highly decentralized process triggered by colony growth and timed to maximize survival of both swarms and the home colonies from which they came.

Winston, M.L. and G.W. Otis. "Ages of Bees in Swarms and Afterswarms of the African-ized Honey Bee." *Journal of Apicultural Research*, no. 17 (1978): 123–29.

Winston, M.L. "Intra-colony Demography and Reproductive Rate of the Africanized Honey Bee in South America." *Behavioral Ecology and Sociobiology*, no. 4 (1979): 279–92.

Winston, M.L. and O.R. Taylor. "Factors Preceding Queen Rearing in the Africanized Honeybee in South America." *Insectes Sociaux*, no. 27 (1980): 289–304.

Winston, M.L. "Swarming, Afterswarming and Reproductive Rate of Unmanaged Honeybee Colonies (*Apis mellifera*)." *Insectes Sociaux*, no. 27 (1980): 391–98.

Winston, M.L., O.R. Taylor and G.W. Otis. "Swarming, Colony Growth Patterns, and Bee Management." *The American Bee Journal*, no.120 (1980): 826–30.

Winston, M.L., J. Dropkin and O.R. Taylor. "Demography and Life History Character-istics of Two Honeybee Races (*Apis mellifera*)." *Oecologia*, no. 48 (1981): 407–13.

Lee, P.C. and M.L. Winston. "The Effect of Swarm Size and Date of Issue on Comb Construction in Newly Founded Colonies of Honey Bees (*Apis mellifera* L.)." *Canadian Journal of Zoology*, no. 63 (1985): 524–27.

Lee, P.C. and M.L. Winston. "The Influence of Swarm Population on Brood Production and Emergent Worker Weight in Newly Founded Honey Bee Colonies. (*Apis mellifera*)." *Insectes Sociaux*, no. 32 (1985): 96–103.

Lee, P.C. and M.L. Winston. "Effect of Reproductive Timing and Colony Size on the Survival, Offspring Colony Size, and Drone Production in the Honey Bee (*Apis mellifera*)." *Ecological Entomology*, no. 12 (1987): 187–95.

Naumann, K. and M.L. Winston. "Effect of Swarm Type on Temporal Caste Poly-ethism in the Honey Bee, *Apis mellifera* L. (Hymenoptera: Apidae)." *Insectes Sociaux*, no. 37 (1990): 58–72.

Winston, M.L., H.A. Higo and K.N. Slessor. "The Effect of Various Dosages of Queen Mandibular Pheromone on the Inhibition of Queen Rearing in the Honey Bee (Hymenoptera: Apidae)." *Annals of the Entomological Society of America*, no. 83 (1990): 234–38.

Naumann, K., M.L. Winston, K.N. Slessor. "Movement of Honey Bee (*Apis mellifera* L.) Queen Mandibular Gland Pheromone in Populous and Unpopulous Colonies." *Journal of Insect Behavior*, no. 6 (1993): 211–23.

Mites: A tiny little mite, varroa, has been decimating honeybee colonies throughout the world, as it's been accidentally introduced to country after country over the last thirty years. It was originally identified as *Varroa jacobsoni*, but careful study by an Australian scientist revealed that it was a different, previously unknown species, which he granted the appropriate name of *Varroa destructor*. The mite feeds on pupal and adult bees, but more significantly transmits and activates viruses and generally kills colonies within a year or two of infestation. A second mite, *Acarapis woodi*, lives in the bees' breathing tubes (trachea) and while less catastrophic also causes some damage to colonies.

The first wave of treatments against the mites relied on synthetic chemical pesticides, not ideal in colonies that produced honey for human consumption. And the mites soon became resistant, leading to an escalating pesticide arms race. To get off this treadmill, we studied safer natural substances such as neem oil and various essential oils, some of which have been at least moderately successful at reducing mite populations. If honey is to retain its reputation as a natural, healthy sweetener, perhaps natural substances are more appropriate than manufactured pesticides.

Melathopolous, Adony P., Mark L. Winston, et al. "Comparative Laboratory Toxicity of Neem Pesticides to Honey Bees (Hymenoptera: Apidae), Their Mite Parasites *Varroa jacobsoni* (Acari: Varroidae) and *Acarapis woodi* (Acari: Tarsonemidae), and Brood Pathogens *Paenibacillus larvae* and *Ascophera apis*." *Journal of Economic Entomology*, no. 93 (2000):199–209.

Melathopolous, Adony P., Mark L. Winston, et al. "Field Evaluation of Neem and Canola Oil for the Selective Control of the Honey Bee (Hymenoptera: Apidae) Mite Parasites *Varroa jacobsoni* (Acari: Varroidae) and *Acarapis woodi* (Acari: Tarsonemidae)." *Journal of Economic Entomology*, no. 93 (2000): 559–67.

Whittington, R., Mark L. Winston, et al. "Evaluation of the Botanical Oils Neem, Thymol and Canola Sprayed to Control *Varroa jacobsoni* Oud. (Acari: Varroidae) and *Acarapis woodi* (Acari: Tarsonemidae) in Colonies of Honey Bees (*Apis mellifera* L., Hymenoptera: Apidae)." *The American Bee Journal*, no. 140 (2000): 567–72.

Packaging Bees: Colonies can have up to two-thirds of their worker bees removed in the spring, shaken into packages and shipped long distances, yet recover by the end of the season to be almost indistinguishable from colonies with no bees removed. The key is resilience, the ability of colonies to call on reserve bees that only up their work pace when colonies are threatened or opportunities arise.

Winston, M.L., S.R. Mitchell and E.N. Punnett. "Feasibility of Package Honey Bee (Hymenoptera: Apidae) Production in Southwestern British Columbia, Canada." *Journal of Economic Entomology*, no. 78 (1985): 1037–41.

Winston, M.L. and S.R. Mitchell. "The Timing of Package Honey Bee (Hymenoptera: Apidae) Production and Use of Two–queen Management in Southwestern British Columbia, Canada." *Journal of Economic Entomology*, no. 79 (1986): 952–56.

Winston, M.L. and L.A. Fergusson. "The effect of worker loss on temporal caste structure in colonies of the honey bee (*Apis mellifera* L.)." *Canadian Journal of Zoology*, no. 63 (1985): 777–80.

Tenczar, P., C. Lutz, V. Rao, N. Goldenfeld and G. Robinson. "Automated Monitoring Reveals Extreme Interindividual Variation and Plasticity in Honeybee Foraging Activity Levels." *Animal Behaviour*, no. 95 (2014): 41–8.

Fragments, QMP and Queenright: Honeybee colonies have a cohesion factor, queen pheromone, which is the magic glue turning tens of thousands of individuals into a colony. My laboratory, in intimate collaboration with my chemistry colleague Keith Slessor and his students, identified nine components of this complex blend over two decades of research. We also confirmed that it is picked up by workers that surround, lick and touch the queen in close contact, then move through the nest and pass her pheromone to other workers. In that way, the queen's presence is communicated to the colony, and the diverse functions of the pheromone that influence worker behaviour and physiology are spread through the nest.

Slessor, K.N., M.L. Winston, et al. "Semiochemical Basis of the Retinue Response to Queen Honey Bees." *Nature,* no. 332 (1988): 354–56.

Naumann, K., M.L. Winston, et al. "The Production and Transmission of Honey Bee Queen (*Apis mellifera L.*) Mandibular Gland Pheromone." *Behavioral Ecology and Sociobiology,* no. 29 (1991): 321–32.

Winston, M.L. and K.N. Slessor. "An Essence of Royalty: Honey Bee Queen Pheromone." *American Scientist,* no. 80 (1992): 374–85

Lin, Huarong, M.L. Winston, et al. "Influence of Age and Population Size on Ovarian Development and of Trophallaxis on Ovarian Development and Vitellogenin Titres of Queenless Worker Honey Bees (Hymenoptera: Apidae)." *Canadian Entomologist,* no 131 (1999): 695–706.

Keeling, Chris I., Mark L. Winston, et al. "New Components of the Honey Bee (*Apis mellifera L.*) Queen Retinue Pheromone." *Proceedings of the National Academy of Sciences of the United States of America,* no. 100 (2003): 4486–91.

Ovaries: Science is about materials and methods long before it's about results. The development of honeybee worker ovaries has been a subject of great fascination to scientists because worker bees have the capacity to lay eggs but rarely develop their ovaries in the presence of their queen. But other factors also influence worker ovaries, and to study those we had to develop methods of measuring ovary size and protein content, and ways to carefully expose worker bees to particular ages and populations of other bees.

Lin, Huarong, M.L. Winston, et al. "Influence of Age and Population Size on Ovarian Development and of Trophallaxis on Ovarian Development and Vitellogenin Titres of Queenless Worker Honey Bees (Hymenoptera: Apidae)." *Canadian Entomologist*, no. 131 (1999): 695–706.

Elizabeth J. Duncan, Otto Hyink and Peter K. Dearden. "Notch Signalling Mediates Reproductive Constraint in the Adult Worker Honeybee." *Nature Communications*, no. 7 (2016): 124–27.

Blueberry: There are over a hundred species of wild bees in the Fraser Valley of British Columbia, where most of western Canada's high bush blueberries are grown, but heavy pesticide use by farmers has reduced their populations to the point where growers have to rent managed honeybee colonies and have them moved into flowering blueberries each year to pollinate the crop. Our research revealed that wild bees were not present in sufficient diversity and abundance to pollinate, but also that synthetic honeybee queen pheromone sprayed on blueberries during bloom enhanced pollination by attracting higher numbers of honeybees to the crop.

Currie, R.W., M.L. Winston and K.N. Slessor. "Impact of Synthetic Queen Mandibular Pheromone Sprays on Honey Bee (*Apis mellifera* L.) Pollination of Berry Crops." *Journal of Economic Entomology*, no. 85 (1992): 1300–06.

Higo, H., M.L. Winston and K.N. Slessor. "Mechanisms by Which Honeybee (Hymenoptera: Apidae) Queen Pheromone Sprays Enhance Pollination." *Annals of the Entomological Society of America*, no. 88 (1995): 366–73.

MacKenzie, K.E. and M.L. Winston. "Diversity and Abundance of Native Bee Pollinators on Berry Crops and Natural Vegetation in the Lower Fraser Valley, BC." *Canadian Entomologist*, no. 116 (1984): 965–74.

Winston, M.L. and K.N. Slessor. "An Essence of Royalty: Honey Bee Queen Pheromone." *American Scientist*, no. 80 (1992): 374–85.

Bees in the City: We studied the diversity and abundance of wild bees in the city of Vancouver, testing our hypothesis that feral solitary and bumblebee populations would be diminished in an urban habitat. To our surprise, we found the opposite; bees were quite diverse and abundant, thriving in the disrupted ecosystems that characterize most cities, including Vancouver.

Tommasi, Désirée, Mark L. Winston, et al. "Bee Diversity and Abundance in an Urban Setting." *Canadian Entomologist*, no. 136 (2004): 851–69.

ACKNOWLEDGEMENTS

To Lori Bamber, who among other things first saw the possibility of a book. Her insightful personality, compassionate disposition and love inhabit every page.

I am also grateful beyond words to the 115 co-authors of my scientific publications, as well as the many research assistants and colleagues who may not have made it to author status but nevertheless contributed to the research. Many of you have become close friends, and all enriched my life beyond measure.

Zachary Finkelstein, son-in-law extraordinaire, kindly enlightened me about symphonic structure. Richard Hoshino, mathematician and novelist, instructed me about the proper way to express percentage increase.

Thank you to Tracey Smith for suggesting I read Frank C. Pellet's 1938 book *History of American Beekeeping* for information about the Roots and the early history of package bee production.

And to Renée, appreciation for sharing your poetic persona and enthusiasm for the bees, and for inspiring me to revisit work I thought I had left behind.

—Mark L. Winston

Gratitude, as always, to my husband, who helps makes my poetic practice possible and thanks to: Chris Turnbull & that long line of poets, dancers, makers; the gardeners and bee-keepers of Joyce-Collingwood and the parks of the City of Vancouver; the writing-work of Leanne Simpson, Jane Jacobs, Sara Ahmed, Mary Louise Pratt and Rebecca Schneider; the poems of Emily Dickinson and M.NourbeSe Philip; the poetry and essays included in issues of *The Carnegie Newsletter*; Paul Taylor, editor; the work of Fred Wah, especially *Pictograms from the Interior of BC* and an essay I wrote about Jordan Abel's poem, "rival trading places," published in *Line Break*.

That afternoon, upstairs in the music room: Satyajit Ray, *The Music Room*; *The Letters of John Keats*, Oxford University Press, 1935 (edited by Maurice Buxton Forman); all the open access science papers available on the internet, for example, Franceso Nazzi's "The hexagonal shape of the honey comb," Robert L.

Jeanne's "Behaviour During Swarm Movement in *Stelopolybia areata*," Michael S. Engle, Jaime Ortega-Blanco, Paul C. Nasimbene and Hukam Singh's "The bees of Early Eocene Cambay amber" and D.M. Mate and Makde's "Pollen of *Apis* honey from Maharashtra, Bhusari, N.V."

The editors and compilers of *Digital Dante*; the art, writings and research of Jasna Guy, Lori Weidenhammer, Brian Campbell and Nancy Holmes; Mark, who gave me his ticket so that I might attend an exhibition curated by Nan Capogna at the Richmond Art Gallery in September of 2015; Bruce Archibald for his email correspondence as well as "Early Eocene insects from Quilchena, British Columbia, and their paleoclimatic implications," and finally, gratitude to Mark for open access to his research papers.

—Renée Sarojini Saklikar

We are deeply grateful to our colleagues at Nightwood Editions, who have been a real delight to collaborate with on this book. Silas White provided astute editorial comments and was instrumental in combining our voices into an effective format. Amber McMillan also contributed her editorial expertise, and Carleton Wilson provided the inspired cover and book design. We are also grateful to Annie Boyar for her fine work as our publicist extraordinaire.

Appreciation to the Atwal family for a donation in support of this project, in memory of Dr. A.S. Atwal.

—Mark L. Winston and Renée Sarojini Saklikar

NOTES

A version of "Competing Doomsdays" first appeared in *Bee Culture*.

A shorter version of "Bee Audacious" was part of the final report for the Bee Audacious Conference.

Earlier iterations of the essay and poems in "Apples and Honey" and "À Moishe (to Mark)" first appeared in *Sustenance Anthology*.

PHOTO CREDIT: SFU

PHOTO CREDIT: SANDRA VANDER SCHAAF

ABOUT THE AUTHORS

MARK L. WINSTON'S *BEE TIME: LESSONS FROM THE HIVE* RECEIVED THE 2015 Governor General's Literary Award for non-fiction. One of the world's leading experts on bees and pollination, Dr. Winston is also an internationally recognized researcher, teacher and writer. He directed Simon Fraser University's Centre for Dialogue for twelve years where he founded the Centre's Semester in Dialogue, a program that creates leadership development opportunities that equip and empower students to contribute to social change in communities.

As a consultant, Dr. Winston partners with universities, corporations, NGOs, governments and communities to advance communication skills, engage public audiences with controversial issues through dialogue, and implement experiential learning and community engagement in educational institutions. As an award-winning writer and editor, he works with students, scientists, other professionals and writers to develop compelling non-fiction. Dr. Winston is a Professor and Senior Fellow at Simon Fraser University's Centre for Dialogue, and a Professor of Biological Sciences. He lives in Vancouver, BC.

RENÉE SAROJINI SAKLIKAR IS POET LAUREATE FOR THE CITY OF SURREY, British Columbia. Passionate about connecting people through poetry, as Laureate in Surrey, Renée offers free writing consultations, teaches poetry in schools and at community events and hosts workshops with youth and seniors to tell Surrey stories (*Surrey Stories Connect: teens and seniors write Surrey*, Surrey Libraries, 2016).

Trained as a lawyer at the University of British Columbia with a degree in English Literature, Renée teaches creative writing for Simon Fraser University and Vancouver Community College. Renée's first book, *children of air india*, (Nightwood Editions, 2013) won the 2014 Canadian Authors Association Award for poetry and her second book with Wayde Compton, *The Revolving City: 51 Poems and the Stories Behind Them* (Anvil Press/SFU Public Square, 2015) was a finalist for a 2016 City of Vancouver Book Award. Fascinated by artistic collaboration, Renée's work has been made into opera and song cycles (*air india [redacted]*, Turning Point Ensemble, 2015) and visual art (Chris Turnbull, see *thecanadaproject* on Wordpress for images from Turnbull's outdoor eco-installation featuring Renée's poetry).

Renée is working on an epic sci-fi journey poem, "THOT-J-BAP," parts of which appear in literary journals (*The Capilano Review, Dusie, The Rusty Toque, Tripwire*) and chapbooks (above/ground, Nous-zot and Nomados presses) and her chapbook, *After the Battle of Kingsway, the bees,* was a finalist for the 2017 bpNichol chapbook award. She has recently published a long poem about her personal connection to the Air India Flight 182 bombing, in an anthology of scholarly and artistic work (*Remembering Air India, the art of public mourning,* University of Alberta Press, 2017). Renée lives in Vancouver, BC.